AF893221

# More Incredible Hawaii

# More Incredible Hawaii

Text by Terence Barrow
Illustrations by Ray Lanterman

CHARLES E. TUTTLE COMPANY, INC.
Rutland Vermont: Tokyo Japan

*Representatives:*

*For Continental Europe:*
BOXERBOOKS, INC., *Zurich*
*For the British Isles:*
PRENTICE-HALL INTERNATIONAL, INC., *London*
*For Australasia:*
BOOKWISE,
*1 Jeanes Street, Beverly, 5009, South Australia*

Published by the Charles E. Tuttle Company, Inc.
of Rutland, Vermont & Tokyo, Japan
with editorial offices at
Suido 1-chome, 2-6, Bunkyo-ku, Tokyo



Library of Congress Catalog Card No. 85-051112
International Standard Book No. 0-8048-1427-9

First Printing, 1985

Printed in U.S.A.

# Table of Contents

# Publisher's Foreword

THIS BOOK IS THE FRUIT OF A COLLABORATION BETWEEN author-anthropologist Terence Barrow and artist-illustrator Ray Lanterman. It is a worthy successor to their INCREDIBLE HAWAII published by the Charles E. Tuttle Company in 1974. The first book was received with enthusiasm by tourists, residents, and school readers of various grades. Teachers said it enlivened Hawaiian history.

The fifty-two illustrated essays of MORE INCREDIBLE HAWAII, are even more fascinating than the first series. The convenient format chosen by the publisher is again that of the standard Tut Book noted for high quality paper and presentation. MORE INCREDIBLE HAWAII is an admirable companion to INCREDIBLE HAWAII and should receive the same enthusiastic reception.

Author and artist have drawn subjects from their extensive knowledge of Hawaii's past. Both men have the advantage of long residence in Hawaii with personal contact with the Hawaiian people, local scholars, and institutions. It is evident they know and love these islands. Also, they appreciate the unique qualities of Hawaii. What other land is isolated from continents by thousands of miles of ocean on all sides? Where else was such a lavish stone age culture ruled by divine chiefs and their priestly advisors? Where else is there such a rich history that includes a cavalcade of maritime explorers, missionaries, sandalwood traders, whalers, enterprising beachcombers and nut-brown maidens? Many highlights of Hawaii's enthralling story are related here in language all can understand.

# Acknowledgements

AUTHOR AND ARTIST REQUIRED LITTLE "OUTSIDE HELP" in forming this book as they both turned to their extensive knowledge of Hawaii, their files and private libraries. Between them there existed a happy collaboration and interchange of ideas. However, acknowledgements must be made where due. June Bradley provided information on Honolulu's mission houses. Napua Stevens, an authority on "Night Marchers" explained that fascinating subject. Jean Dodge and her daughter Susan Rowe took on the onerous task of primary editing, and typing of the manuscript. Their cheerful help and encouragement is appreciated by both author and artist.

# 1 The Creation of Polynesian Man

HAWAIIANS SHARE A CULTURE WITH ALL THE POLYNESIANS living on islands of the triangle marked at its corners by Hawaii, New Zealand, and Easter Island. In Polynesia there are many versions of how mankind was created. The idea of a primal Sky Father and an Earth Mother who gave birth to male gods, who in turn made men and women, is universal. In the Hawaiian story, the Sky Father, Wakea, and the Earth Mother, Papa (or Haumea), were locked in an embrace, floating in the cosmic night called Po. After billions of years, the earth and all living creatures were created. The process is expressed in the Hawaiian chant named the Kumulipo. Polynesian ideas of evolution are remarkably close to modern scientific concepts.

In due time, the primal parents gave birth to many gods. The chief deity, Kane, excelled others in wisdom and creativeness. Next was Ku, who looked after matters of war, male generative power, sorcery, and growth in nature. Lono, an immigrant from the far land of Kahiki, presided over agriculture, fertility, and clouds and winds. Kanaloa, the fourth of the great gods, became god of the sea.

Kane created various plants and animals, and he made the first man from red clay mixed with his spittle. With the aid of Ku and Lono, he breathed life into this image in his own likeness. This Polynesian Adam, named Kumuhonua, had a beautiful maiden named Lalohonua made from his side as he slept. Unfortunately, like the Biblical Adam and Eve, they disobeyed divine law and lost their immortality as offspring of the gods.

RAY
LANTERMAN

# 2 How Maui Made the Day Longer

All Polynesians, of whom the Hawaiians are an extended family, had their stories of gods and heroes just as the Greeks, Egyptians, and other peoples of the world. Their demi-god, the trickster Maui, stands out above all others for superhuman feats. He fished up islands from the sea bed, but his achievement of snaring the sun to make the day longer is his most famous deed.

According to this Pacific-wide legend, gods and humans alike complained that the sun moved too rapidly across the heavens. It did not allow them time to complete their daily tasks. Maui, son of the goddess Hina of the Moon, decided it was time the sun was taught a lesson. He made many ropes from coconuts by rolling the husk fibers on his thigh, then braiding the cords together. His companions laughed at him, saying it was a hopeless task.

When all was ready, Maui climbed to the peak of the great volcano Haleakala to await the sun's ascent. In due time the glow in the east told Maui of the rising of the sun so he carefully laid out his coconut fiber ropes. When the sun had climbed high enough, he cast his snare into the air and caught his quarry. The sun was infuriated, but Maui beat it with ferocity and with dire threats that so intimidated the sun he agreed to move more slowly in the future. So the day was made long enough for mankind to work at leisure in daylight hours. The island of Maui is named after this demi-god hero.

RAY
LANTERMAN

# 3 Gods of Old Hawaii

When the Polynesians ventured to Hawaii from East Polynesia about a thousand years ago they brought with them religious ideas. They had already gods, ancestral guardians, and spirit powers, which they depicted in sculptures of wood and stone.

There were four principal gods. They were Kane, who managed matters of creation, sunlight, forests, and fresh water. Ku, the red god of war, thirsted for bloody sacrifice. Lono was the diety of peaceful pursuits and earthly fertility. Kanaloa cared for the affairs of the sea.

Only trained priests communicated with these great gods. The common men and women had their ancestral and guardian spirits, some taking the form of owls, sharks, lizards, and other creatures, but the affairs of the supreme gods were the concern of elite professionals.

In 1819 King Kamehameha II (Liholiho), the son of Kamehameha the Great, decreed that the old Hawaiian religion be abandoned and that its temples and images be destroyed. Hawaiian traditional religion came to an end, yet practitioners of it still exist to this day. Many old images have been found in caves and hidden places where they were placed by Hawaiians who, it seems, were not prepared to destroy the sacred vehicles of their gods and ancestral spirits.

At the top left is an image of the sorcery god Kalaipahoa. At upper right is a representation of the war god Ku. Below left is a peg-like god of unknown name held by a priest. On the lower right is a female goddess believed to represent the fire-volcano goddess Pele.

RAY
LANTERMAN

# 4 Temples of War and Peace

THROUGHOUT THE HAWAIIAN ISLANDS THERE ARE MANY man-made piles of stones which are the bases of temples built to honor the gods. A few of the temples have been restored to something of their former appearance with replicas of images and thatched structures. For example, at Honaunau on the Big Island of Hawaii there are such restorations.

Visitors to Kailua town will find opposite the wharf and adjoining the grounds of the King Kamehameha Hotel the restoration of the Ahu'ena heiau (heiau is the Hawaiian word for temple).

Kamehameha, having succeeded in unifying the Hawaiian Islands into one kingdom, decided to live out his golden years at Kailua. About 1812 he reconstructed this old temple which had existed on the site for centuries before his birth. When he died on May 8, 1819, Kamehameha was secretly buried. He had never accepted the Christian faith, although informed about it by many early visitors, including Captain Cook and Captain Vancouver. He stuck to traditional Hawaiian beliefs. The Ahu'ena heiau was to him a sacred place of sacrifice and worship. Today, it is predominantly a tourist curiousity, yet to those who know of such matters the spirits still lurk there. All should treat the place with reverence. There is a brooding presence of 'something' at this place, even when it is in the bright Hawaiian sunlight.

AHUENA HEIAU, *Kailua-Kona, Island of Hawaii*

# 5 Maiden of the Rainbow

ABOVE BUSTLING WAIKIKI, WITH ITS ANNUAL COUNT OF millions of tourist visitors, is the verdant and peaceful Manoa valley. At its head the high ridges of the Ko'olau Range form an impassable barrier where, after rains, waterfalls drop down. The tradewinds sweeping over the ridges bring showers and mists. The sun glints from droplets of moisture to form rainbows. It is a romantic valley with many romantic legends. Dwarf-men haunt the night – the so-called Menehune.

The most famous supernatural dweller of Manoa Valley is the Rainbow Maiden. This goddess is called Kahala-o-Puna or for brevity, Kahala and she shall be so named here. Kahala had arching over her a rainbow which moved with her as she wandered about the valley.

Two young Hawaiian chiefs desired this lovely girl. One, named Kauhi, lived at nearby Waikiki. He was a descendant of the shark god, so had a cruel streak. The second suitor, a handsome chief, lived between Waikiki and Manoa and was a kind and loving man.

Kauhi became angry with Kahala because of jealousy, killed her, then buried her body. Kahala's owl guardian dug her up and restored her to life by magic power. Kauhi killed her again, this time burying her under a tree where the roots prevented her from being dug up by the owl spirit. Her true love, searching for her, saw a rainbow over her grave. He exhumed her and by magic she was again restored to her youthful radiance, rainbow and all. They married and lived happily ever after. The wicked Kauhi met his fate by being cooked alive in his own earth oven.

KE ANUENUE
ANUENUE KAU PO
Lunar Rainbow
RAY LANTERMAN

# 6 Pele, the Goddess of Fire and Volcanoes

THE OLD-TIME HAWAIIANS HAD NUMEROUS GODS, GODDESSES, and ancestral guardians. There were spirits of earth, sea, and air that were loved or feared, according to their character. One supernatural spirit is very much alive today in the minds of the living. She is the goddess of fire and volcanoes, the great Madame Pele. Pele, who arrived in the Hawaiian Islands as an immigrant, fought a successful battle with the goddess of ice and snow.

Pele proceeded to create Hawaiian landscape features as she moved about. Today she dwells, it is said, in the firepit of Halema'uma'u in Kilauea crater on the slopes of Mauna Loa, active in pouring forth red molten lava. When she is manifestly angry, residents to this day direct pleas to her and make ritual offerings. For example Hilo town, constantly threatened with obliteration by flows of lava, has good reason to placate Madame Pele.

Pele can be kind and warmhearted when she is pleased. Reports are often made of her appearances in the guise of a beautiful young girl, a wrinkled hag, a playful child, or a small white dog. Those who are kind and helpful benefit, while the niggardly or inhospitable suffer. Some say she begs rides on Hawaii's highways, then, after entering an automobile, disappears.

Pele is thus both beloved and feared. She was born of flame in the mouth of the Earth Mother Haumea. Her younger sister, Hi'iaka, goddess of hula art, is called upon in chants by hula dancers. Visitors should be wary of Pele. Never pluck her sacred red ohi'a blossoms or her red ohelo berries without due ritual. Pele expects recognition and some small offering should be made to her.

RAY
LANTERMAN

# 7 Hawaiian "Hotspot" of Island Births

THIS GLOBE ON WHICH WE LIVE WAS, UNTIL RECENTLY, considered a rigid ball with an unmoving surface. Its annual journey around the sun was obvious. What was not recognized until recently is that the surface of the earth has vast plates that float about at the rate of a few inches a year as they glide on the molten substance of the earth's mantle.

Hawaii is on the "Pacific plate" which has for millions of years drifted northwest in the direction of the Asian mainland. The Hawaiian chain of islands stretches out in that general direction. The oldest of them have worn down to mere reefs or rocky islets. Rain and sea waves erode all lands, in due time.

Kaua'i, the oldest inhabited island, is now half its original height. It was formed as an active volcano as were the others. Hawaii, which stands over thirteen thousand feet above sea level is still in the process of building by the outpouring of lava from its active volcano.

As the Pacific plate slowly drifts to the northwest it passes over what is called a "hot spot" where lava wells up from a crust rift. In time, submarine mountains burst above sea level. Most Hawaiian islands are now "dead." Their volcanic activity ceases when they are no longer on or near the hot spot. Maui which is next in line from Hawaii has had an outpouring of lava in the 18th century so it is a dormant rather than extinct volcano. Kaua'i, O'ahu, Lana'i and Moloka'i seem to have long since passed their eruptive phases and are much eroded by rains and sea waves. The "outer islands" to the northwest, beyond Kaua'i and Ni'ihau, are so worn down they are mere rocky islets or reefs.

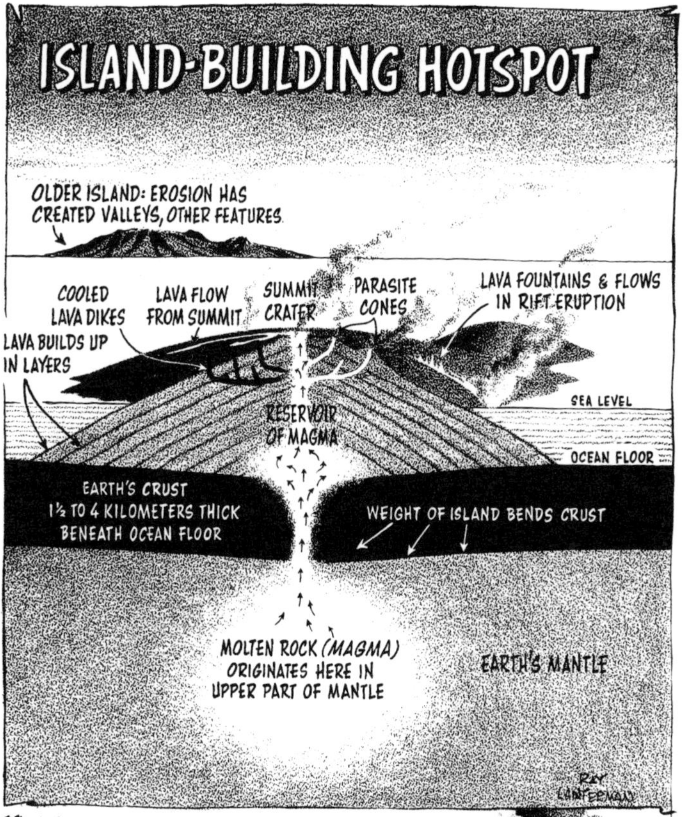


## HOW THE ISLANDS GREW:

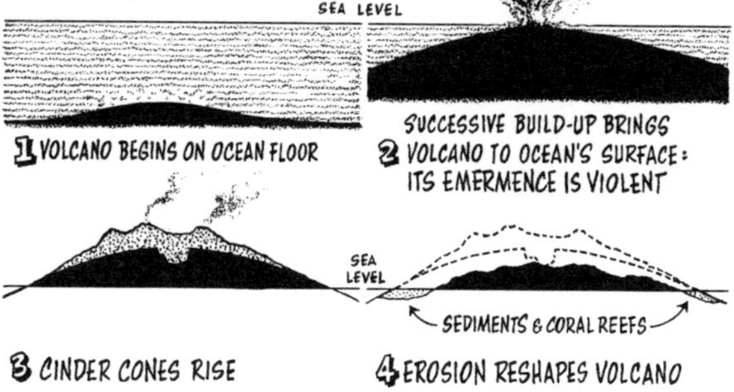


*Diagrams after Stearns & Macdonald*

# 8 The Formation of Maui, "The Valley Isle"

RESIDENTS OF MAUI BELIEVE THAT THEIR ISLAND IS THE happiest in the Hawaiian Islands. They say, "Maui no ka oi," that is, "Maui is the best." Maui is lovely and has a special charm, yet this is true of all the islands. It is quite natural that those native to a place think their home is the best. "Heavenly Hana" on the eastern side of Maui certainly is a place as close to the Garden of Eden that one is likely to find.

Maui was created in the same way as other Hawaiian islands – by the outpouring of lava from the hot spot rift of the ocean floor. As the great Pacific plate on which the island now sits passed over this site – a spot now occupied by Hawaii – the island, like O'ahu, was formed by two submarine volcanoes that rose above the sea millions of years ago, joined together. Between them is an isthmus of flattish land. Over millions of years, erosion cut deep V-shaped canyons into these mountains. In some places, such as about Olowalu near Lahaina, soil and rock washed out of the deep valleys to form sloping coastal plains. This process gave birth to the dramatic and dynamic landscape characteristic of this island.

The West Maui mountains reach up to about six thousand feet. In the east, the larger mountain mass rises to over ten thousand feet. At Haleakala National Park, visitors may see the great craters of the mountain Haleakala, a name meaning "House of the Sun". It was at this place, according to Hawaiian legend, that the demi-god Maui lassoed the sun and thrashed into submission and agreement that it move more slowly across the sky.

EONS AGO: BOILING UP FROM THE OCEAN FLOOR THROUGH THREE MILES OF WATER, FOUR ISLANDS FORMED THE *MAUI GROUP.* IN GLACIAL TIMES, WHEN THE SEA WAS LOWER, ALL FOUR WERE JOINED AS ONE ISLAND—*MAUI NUI.* IT PROBABLY LOOKED LIKE THIS:

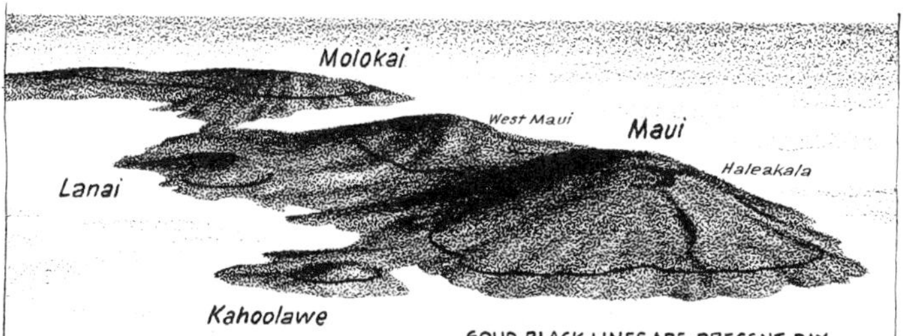


SOLID BLACK LINES ARE PRESENT-DAY SHORELINES

ONE OF MAUI'S SCENIC WONDERS IS IAO *NEEDLE*, WHOSE PEAK RISES TO 2,250 FT.: FROM KEPANIWAI PARK IT APPEARS TO BE AN ISOLATED PINNACLE; IN REALITY THE "NEEDLE" IS A KNOB AT THE BEGINNING OF A LONG RIDGE

RAY LANTERMAN

# 9 Hawaii's First Mammal Residents

HAWAII'S POLYNESIAN SETTLERS BROUGHT WITH THEM DOGS, pigs, and rats. They were greeted by two mammals already resident in Hawaii whose ancestors had been about for tens of thousands of years, namely the indigenous bat and seal.

The Hawaiian hoary bat (*Lasiurus cinereus semotus*) which the Hawaiians call ʻopeʻapeʻa from its fluttering flight, came from North America carried on winds and its own wings. The wingspan of these hardly little creatures range from nine inches to over one foot. The body weight varies with the seasons but it does not exceed an ounce and may be as little as half an ounce. Their gray fur has a reddish tinge with whitish frosted tips, hence the name "hoary."

These little creatures are not readily seen. They feed on insects at sunset near shorelines, over streams, and in forest clearings. Their breeding grounds are concentrated on Hawaii and Kauaʻi from sea level up to several thousand feet. They are solitary, and because they blend with the bushes and trees where they sleep they must be searched for to be found.

The Hawaiian monk seal, *Monachus schauinslandi*, called by Hawaiians ʻilio-holo-i-kauaua ("a dog that runs in rough places"), is one of only two living tropical seals. Like its Caribbean cousin, it is unchanged in form in over millions years. Now an endangered species, the monk seal is protected by state legislation. At one time this animal lived throughout the Hawaiian Islands. The advent of sealers in the early 19th century depleted its numbers. Its slaughter suffered in accessible areas of coast brought the monk seal to near extinction. Today they are found on the rocky shores of islets and the sands of distant reefs. A few of these charming and comical creatures can be seen at the Waikiki Aquarium.

MEET LASIURUS CINEREUS SEMOTUS
-THE FELLOW WHO GOT HERE FIRST
CALLED OPE'APE'A BY THE HAWAIIANS, THE BAT ESTABLISHED A COLONY IN THE ISLANDS EONS BEFORE THE ARRIVAL OF MAN
LIKE ALL HIS RELATIVES, HE SLEEPS HANGING UPSIDE DOWN, BUT PREFERS TREES TO CAVES
ANOTHER OLD-TIMER IS 'ILIO-HOLO-I-KAUAUA
(DOG RUNNING IN THE TOUGH PLACES)
THE MONK SEAL
RAY LANTERMAN

# 10 Kaua'i, Isle of Lonely Loveliness

KAUA'I, NAMED THE "GARDEN ISLAND" IS WITH ITS SISTER island of Ni'ihau (the "Forbidden Island"), the most northwesterly inhabited part of the Hawaiian chain. Kaua'i is an island of unusual charm and fertile beauty. In parts it has a paradisical tropical atmosphere, such as is found about Hanalei Bay and Haena.

It was on this island that Europeans first landed. Captain Cook's ships HMS *Resolution* and HMS *Discovery* anchored off Waimea in 1778 when boats were sent ashore to explore the land.

Kamehameha the Great tried several times to conquer Kaua'i but failed when his fleets were scattered and wrecked by storms. The king of the island of Kaua'i, Kaumuali'i agreed, in 1810, while on a visit to O'ahu where he saw the mounting war canoe fleets, to become Kamehameha's subject. This submission was on the terms that Kaumuali'i live out his days as nominal ruler. Thus the bloodshed of yet another battle of conquest was avoided.

The Russians had long wanted to get a foothold in Hawaii. First they built a blockhouse fort in Honolulu's waterfront in 1816. Kamahameha, fearful of their presence had them ejected. The Russian leader Scheffer withdrew to Kaua'i where he built at Waimea, at the mouth of the river, a larger fort which still stands. In 1816 Kaumuali'i signed a treasonous agreement with the Russians which allowed the Czar Alexander's flag to be raised. For a time Kaua'i was Russian territory. Under pressure from Kamehameha the errant king Kaumuali'i insisted the Russians and their ships depart. Kaumuali'i died in 1824 long after his old enemy Kamehameha had gone to a secret grave.

Kaua'i's eroded sea cliffs and canyons are as spectacular as one can find in the Hawaiian Islands. The island's central mountain Wai'aleale, which stands over 5,000 feet, is said to be the wettest spot on earth with annual rainfall of five to eight hundred inches.

CAPTAIN COOK'S ARRIVAL AT WAIMEA

# 11 Captain Bligh and Hawaii's First Maps

THE NAME CAPTAIN BLIGH BRINGS TO MIND THE 1789 mutiny on His Britannic Majesty's ship *Bounty*. William Bligh, born in Cornwall, England, in 1754, was sailing master with Captain James Cook on HMS *Resolution* when Hawaii was discovered in 1778. Among his duties on *Resolution* was that of handling the ship and charting the coasts of any islands discovered on the voyage.

In his capacity as master he made exact maps and drawings of Hawaii's coasts. He was meticulous, and very concerned with the welfare of men in his charge. On Cook's vessel his authority was limited. There is no record of the outbursts of rage that led to his downfall as captain of *Bounty* and the later rebellion he managed to generate as governor of New South Wales, Australia.

The surveys he made of the islands were excellent. The whereabouts of the original Bligh maps, charts and drawings is considered a mystery yet the simple answer is in the book, *The Life of Vice-Admiral Bligh*, by George Mackaness. The facts are clear and stated in Bligh's own words. When the *Bounty* mutineers forced Bligh into the ship's longboat to be cast adrift, his clerk, a Mr. Samuels, had the sense to gather together things that might be useful. Bligh wrote: "He (Mr. Samuels) attempted to save the time keeper and my maps and drawings, among which were my original surveys of the West Coast of America, and the Sandwich (Hawaiian) and Friendly (Tongan) islands, done when with Captain Cook." These charts were not allowed to go to the ship's boat so they went off with the *Bounty* to Pitcairn Island. There is a remote possibility they have survived, but the chances are they were burnt along with the good ship *Bounty*.

WILLIAM BLIGH
CARTOGRAPHER, SEAMAN EXTRAORDINARY
CAPTAIN, GOVERNOR, AND ADMIRAL
BLIGH AT 36
After a portrait by J. Russell
H.M.S. BOUNTY
RAY LANTERMAN
THE BOUNTY'S LAUNCH IN WHICH BLIGH MANAGED TO REACH TIMOR WAS ONLY 23 FT. LONG AND 6 FT.-9 IN. WIDE. CRAMPED QUARTERS INDEED FOR 19 MEN.

# 12 Stony Wards of Royal Birth

THE HAWAII NOBILITY BELIEVED THAT IF A BABY WERE born at a hallowed place the mana (the psychic power) of the newborn would be strong and enduring. Certain sites determined as auspicious were marked by groups of stones.

Fortunately, two of the most famous "royal birthstone" clusters are still intact. One, "Pohaku Ho'ohanau," is in the temple complex of Ka-lae-o-ka-manu adjacent to the outlet of the Wailua River on Kaua'i. The other, named "Kukaniloko" after some noble woman of past times, is on O'ahu on the high plain between the Ko'olau and Wai'anae mountains. These birthstones are situated in a Wahiawa pineapple field adjacent to the highway and may be reached by a short field road passing through a pineapple field.

The Kukaniloko birthstones, dating from the 12th century A.D., were inaugurated by a ruler named Nanakaoko, whose wife Kahihiokalana gave birth there to Kapawa, who became a ruling chief. The stones became imbued with great magical power. In 1797, King Kamehameha the Great wished his sacred wife, Keopuolani, to give birth to their child there but the queen was too ill to travel from the "Big Island" of Hawaii. Thus, their son, Kamehameha II (Liholiho), missed the auspicious blessing of the place. In fact, he was ill-fated, as he died in London in 1824 at an early age, along with his queen, Kamamalu, both of measles.

RAY
LANTERMAN

# 13 Destruction of an Army By Volcanic Eruption

VISITORS TO THE BIG ISLAND MAY NOTICE AS THEY PASS along the Mamalahoa Highway of the Ka'u District a guidepost that indicates a trail where there are footprints believed to have been impressed into the ash when Keoua's army was overwhelmed by a volcanic eruption in 1790. Keoua was the son of Kalaniopu'u, Hawaii's ruling chief who died in 1782. Keoua was not happy with the land inheritance granted him, so he joined his brother Kiwalao to fight against Kamehameha, who was already embarked on his ambitious plan to conquer all Hawaiian islands.

For a time, Keoua was successful in taking land and in the process killed a rather overbearing uncle named Keawemauhili. He then invaded the northern parts of Hawaii while Kamehameha was off fighting elsewhere. All might have gone well but as his army of about four hundred warriors with their families, was returning to Ka'u after conquering Hilo, they were caught by a volcanic eruption. Poisonous gasses suffocated some while falling rocks killed others. Few escaped the devastation and so Keoua's ambitions of conquest were put to an end.

In 1791 Keoua visited Kamehameha's temple at Kawaihae where he was promptly speared to death along with those with him. His body was placed on the sacrificial altar. Kiwalao, his brother, had died in battle the previous year. Thus Kamehameha became the undisputed ruler of the island of Hawaii. All that remains of Keoua's army are footprints in the ashes.

# THE AWFUL DAY WHEN FATE DESTROYED KEOUA'S ARMY

AS THEY TRIED TO FLEE THE HOLOCAUST SOME LEFT FOOTPRINTS WHICH YOU CAN SEE TODAY IN KA'U

# 14 An English Sailor Who Became a High Chief

Behind the Gothic chapel at the Royal Mausoleum at Nu‘uanu, not far above Honolulu, rests in a quiet grave one of the most remarkable figures of Hawaiian history. The person is John Young, who died in 1835. Named Olohana by the Hawaiians he was made a high chief, a rank further elevated by his marriage to Kaonaeha, a niece of Kamehameha. Children were born of the union and the descendants live on to this day. One granddaughter became a royal monarch, Queen Emma.

John Young was an Englishman employed as boatswain of a small furtrader vessel named *Eleanora*. When in Hawaiian waters, the ship was attacked off Maui and the captain, a man named Metcalf, slaughtered many Hawaiians with cannon. In retaliation, his small attendant vessel, the *Fair American*, commanded by his eighteen-year-old son, was attacked and only one sailor, the English youth named Isaac Davis, was allowed to live.

When word reached Kamehameha of this attack with slaughter of crewmen he was furious, as he was cultivating the goodwill of visiting Europeans. Fearful that word of the attack would reach the ears of the terrible Captain Metcalf Kamehameha prevented John Young, who was on shore leave, from returning to his ship.

King Kamehameha gathered European advisors. None were more valued or more trusted than John Young and Isaac Davis. Both men aided Kamehameha in his wars of conquest, as strategists and as operators of cannon. Young lived out his life quite happily in his adoptive home. The England of his youth was a place where poverty and hard labor were the lot of most men, women and children. It is little wonder that he was content to live out his days as an honored Hawaiian chief.

After an Engaving by Pellion
CAPTAIN COOK "DISCOVERED" THE ISLANDS — ANOTHER ENGLISHMAN -
JOHN YOUNG -
HELPED KAMEHAMEHA UNITE AND GOVERN THEM
RAY LANTERMAN

# 15 The Story of Kamehameha's Statues

A STATUTE OF KING KAMEHAMEHA THE GREAT STANDS in Honolulu in front of the Judiciary Building (Ali'ilani Hale) across from Iolani Palace. Tourists photograph it constantly. It must be the most photographed object in Hawaii. Few know that this statue is not the original one or that it commemorates the centennial of the discovery by Captain James Cook of the Hawaiian Islands in 1778.

The original statue stands before the courthouse in Kohala on the Big Island of Hawaii. Thomas R. Gould, a Boston sculptor who had a studio in Italy, received $10,000 appropriated by King Kalakaua's legislature in 1879 to create the statue. He worked from photographs of a handsome Hawaiian named Robert Hoapili Baker dressed in cape and helmet. A sketch of Kamehameha, made by artist Louis Choris with the Russian expedition of 1816 provided a portrait. The statue's pose is like that of a Roman general with palm held upward to the heavens – the Hawaiians turned the palm downwards in ceremonial appeals to the gods so the pose is not appropriate. However the figure was duly cast in bronze in Paris, then shipped from Bremen, Germany, in the bark *G. F. Haendel.* On the journey to Hawaii the ship was wrecked in the Faulkland Islands near the tip of South America. A resident of Port Stanley salvaged the sculpture which he set up as a novelty.

Unaware that the original statue was still in existence the Hawaii Legislature ordered a replacement using insurance money from the loss. The new statue duly arrived, being made from the mold of the first and was unveiled in Honolulu in 1883.

A Captain Jervis of the ship *Earl Dalhousie* purchased the original statue for $500 while visiting the Faulkland Islands then carried it on to Honolulu where he sold it at a profit. The happy ending is that this first statue was erected before the court house at Kohala, north Hawaii, as a monument to Kamehameha in the place of his birth.

KAMEHAMEHA . I

# 16 Ghost Warriors of the Night

THE HAWAIIAN ISLANDS HAVE, AS MOST PACIFIC ISLANDS, ghostly powers that sometimes show themselves to the living. They appear day and night in valleys, hills, on lava fields, and in forests. Some are heard, some felt as presences, some are seen.

The "Night Marchers" or Huaka'i-po, as the Hawaiians call them, are bands of armed spirit warriors, some clothed with helmets and cloaks, who march on old trails leading from inland to the sea. These processions occur mostly at night, yet it is said they may be seen in broad daylight. When they move along, drums sound and the leader is said to cry out a warning to anyone in their path. Traditional practice advises a quick retreat or a respectful crouch to the ground if they are encountered.

Why these ghostly marchers still make their way from place to place is unclear. Some say it is to visit old battle grounds or to greet visiting clansman. They seem to act as guides in escorting chiefly spirits. A number of men and women in modern Hawaii have described these "Night Marches." Hawaiians regard them as harbingers of death and that some kin of the person who sees or hears them shall die. These ghostly marchers are reputed to kill any humans they find in their path. The prescribed advice is to hide when they are first perceived. Imaginative as these apparitions may seem this writer knows more than one Hawaiian who encountered the fearful marchers of the night.

RAY
LANTERMAN

# 17 Hawaii's Fearsome Ghost Dogs

HAWAIIANS DID NOT SEPARATE THE WORLDS OF HUMAN and animal creation. Everything animate and inanimate had its spirit part. Ghosts existed everywhere. Sharks, owls, and birds served as supernatural guardians of the living and were so venerated.

Dogs, called ‘ilio, were brought to these islands by the Polynesian settlers, who came in their sailing canoes around a thousand years ago. They were both companions and a source of flesh food. As men ate dogs in this world, some dogs became cannibalistic dog-men to haunt misty valleys and to trouble the living with their ghostly barking.

A dog-man named Kaupe is said to haunt the Nu‘uanu Valley above Honolulu. His shadowy body is at times seen in the clouds that linger above the mountains or in the mists that drift down the valley.

Behind the Royal Mausoleum in the lower Nu‘uanu Valley above Honolulu town are petroglyph dog figures pecked on the rocky outcrop of a gulch. No one knows what these dogs represent, yet it is possible they depict the ghost dogs of Nu‘uanu, as they are located in the valley where such spirits linger. Madame Pele the Fire Goddess is said to take the form of a small white dog and indeed the appearances of this little creature under unusual circumstances have often been reported. A tradition on the island of Hawaii is that the appearance of this little fellow on the Saddle Road foretells an eruption of the volcano.

RAY
LANTERMAN

# 18 Pearl Harbor's Shark Goddess

PEARL HARBOR O'AHU, BECAME KNOWN WORLDWIDE WHEN Japan attacked the Pacific Fleet there on December 7, 1941. This waterway, called "Wai Momi" by the Hawaiians, got its historical name because pearl oysters were found there in abundance.

Before the arrival of European ships Hawaiian canoes had glided over its calm waters for centuries. The English ship *Butterworth*, under Captain William Brown, entered Honolulu Harbor in 1793. Pearl Harbor remained neglected by foreign visitors.

In 1877, when Hawaii was still a kingdom, rights to Pearl Harbor were granted to the United States. It was acquired as a coaling place for the new steamships yet it was little used until 1902 when coral rock was blasted away and sand and rock dredged to allow sizeable vessels to enter the locks. Such violent interferences with this realm of the shark goddess Ka'ahupahau made the Hawaiians apprehensive. Predictions of trouble were made, and as harbor work continued there were in fact many accidents, injuries to workers, and general delays. A dredge sank in mid-channel.

When work was started on a drydock, in 1909, over caves where the Hawaiians said the shark goddess and her son, Kahi'uka, lived, dire misfortune was foreseen. So it was in 1913, when the drydock was almost complete. Collapse of the supporting casings caused the sea to rush in to destroy four years of work.

In response to Hawaiian advice, a priest or kahuna was called in to placate the angered shark goddess. When the debris of the fallen dock walls were cleared away the skeleton of an enormous shark was found at the foundations. This discovery caused speculation among the Hawaiians as to its meaning. They asked, "Is this the body of the shark goddess or her son?" Whatever the case, the chants and ritual offerings were successful. Work proceeded without mishap until the dock was completed in 1919.

PEARL HARBOR'S INDUSTRIAL SECTION IN 1919, SHORTLY AFTER THE DRYDOCK, *LOWER LEFT*, WAS COMPLETED

FROM A U S NAVY PHOTO

RAY LANTERMAN

# 19 Guilt in Shaking Water

THE REV. WILLIAM ELLIS, AN ENGLISH MISSIONARY WHO lived in Hawaii in the early 1820s, had the gift of impartiality. While his colleagues were criticizing Hawaiian customs he quietly recorded them in his notebooks. The *Journal of William Ellis* remains one of the best sources on Hawaiian culture and it ranks next in authority to the observations of Captain James Cook.

Ellis, while noting the blessing of the absence of lawyers in old Hawaii, told of a means of determining guilt or innocence by the remarkable process of "wai haruru," a trial which may be interpreted as "shaking water." A bowl of water was brought before the accused who was surrounded by a circle of witnesses. The person held out both hands with fingers spread apart over the water container. A priest who acted as judge watched the water intently for any rippling or disturbance of its surface. If this happened the accused was pronounced guilty and duly punished. No doubt any quivering of the fingers or shaking of the hands suggested guilt but it was the surface of the water that was studied, not the hands.

Another test using a bowl of water was one aimed at detecting the presence of malicious ghosts and of destroying them. The Hawaiians believed that ill health and misfortune were the work of evil spirits sent by sorcerers to harm individuals. In this case the surface of the smooth water was watched closely for the reflection of a ghost face. If one appeared it was grasped at in a way that disturbed the water and so destroyed the reflected image. If the grasping was quick the ghost spirit, whose apparition had appeared on the surface of the water, was destroyed. Such magical practices as these two described served the Hawaiians for many hundreds of years. The psychic and hypnotic powers of the ancient priests, known as kahuna, resulted from long training in arts dealing with the supernatural world.

# KAI HALULU
SHAKING WATER

# 20 Home Sweet Home of Sticks and Grass

MODERN HAWAII HAS A WIDE RANGE OF BUILDINGS made of steel, concrete, wood, glass, and other materials. When Captain Cook visited Hawaii in 1778 and 1779 houses were constructed of wooden posts and poles covered with grass thatching. The smallest dwellings were mere hutches into which a few people crawled for warmth at night or to escape rough weather. Many regions of Hawaiian occupation were not hospitable. Most of the greenery we see today is imported foliage. Chiefly families had fine houses, some of them being quite spacious. Stone foundations and even stone walls were part of the structure of some. There were also temples houses of various uses, canoe houses and so on. Villages were clusters of houses that met many different requirements.

To the earliest European visitors, Hawaiian houses looked like groups of haystacks. Each cluster was neat and served the various needs of village life. Some were reserved for women, others for guests, storage for valuables and other items. Skilled craft workers lashed together notched posts and poles to form the main structure, then grass or leaf thatching was applied. The completion of an important house required a ceremonial opening. A priest cut a grass rope attached to the door which represented an umbilical cord.

The furnishings of all houses were few. The quality and number of the objects usually indicated the rank of the occupants, as the best craft work went to chiefly men and women. Mats, barkcloth bedcovers, plaited pillows, stone lamps, bowls, dishes, fans, and personal items such as clothing were neatly arrayed. Some houses had a stone fireplace for light and warmth. All cooking and eating was done outdoors or under rough shelters.

# THE GRASS HOUSE

IT CAME IN SEVERAL MODELS

IN CONSECRATING A NEW DWELLING, THE KAHUNA "CUT THE HOUSE'S UMBILICAL CORD" BY TRIMMING THE THATCH OVER THE DOORWAY

ITS SIMPLICITY OF FORM IS REFLECTED IN THE ARCHITECTURE OF THE HONOLULU ACADEMY OF ARTS

RAY LANTERMAN

# 21 Bark Cloth of Old Hawaii

HAWAIIANS HAD NO KNOWLEDGE OF WEAVING OR OF woven cloth before the coming of the Europeans. For clothing, bed covers, and other needs, they used bark cloth, called by the common South Sea islands tapa, or the Hawaii, kapa. Hawaiian cloth is the best made and of the most varied in the Pacific islands.

Kapa was made from several plants, according to the intended use of a cloth. The best bark cloth was made from the paper mulberry. Mulberry saplings were harvested by women whose principal craft was kapa-making. They then stripped the bark, broke the saplings into short lengths, and soaked them in water to soften. These soaked pieces were then beaten with a hardwood mallet on a wooden anvil until they spread into flat strips. These strips were then in turn beaten together until they formed felted sheets.

Square-faced beaters carved with surface grooves or patterns left "watermarks" on the finished cloth. Some sheets were further decorated by dyeing or marking by bamboo stamps and cords dipped in pigment. Designs varied. The grades of kapa ranged from cloth of lace-like texture to stiff sheets.

Kapa was used as multilayered waist garments for women. Men usually wore the malo, a narrow length of cloth wrapped around the waist and passed between the legs. The ends of this garment were left to fall down at back and front. Kapa capes, some of which were waterproofed with oils, served when needed.

The ancient Hawaiians were an essentially 'topless' people, the one essential garment was about the waist. High chiefs wore the feathered capes, cloaks, and helmets for ceremonies or war.

TAPA MAKING
TO MAKE TAPA, *Wauke* WAS FIRST SOAKED IN SEA WATER, THEN BEATEN INTO LONG STRIPS: AFTER ANOTHER SOAKING THE STRIPS WERE BEATEN TOGETHER UNTIL THEY ADHERED TO ONE ANOTHER TO FORM A LENGTH OF CLOTH.
USING VEGETABLE DYES AND A CARVED BAMBOO STAMP, THIS GIRL IS DECORATING THE FINISHED PRODUCT
MILADY'S WARDROBE WAS A *Pa'u* OF TAPA
TAPA STAMP CARVED OF WOOD: APPROXIMATELY ACTUAL SIZE
NIPPY WEATHER CALLED FOR A *Kihei* OF TAPA
AND THATCHED CLOAKS KEPT OFF THE RAIN
SANDALS WERE JUST THE THING FOR WALKING ON ROUGH LAVA
RAY LANTERMAN

# 22 Traditional Sports and Leisure Pastimes

MANY RECREATIVE GAMES AND PASTIMES WERE ENJOYED in old Hawaii. Some were intended to teach young men the agility needed in battle. Most were purely games of pleasure indulged in by young and old alike. Surfing, swimming, diving, canoeing were sports still popular today. There is an attempt to revive some traditional Hawaiian games but football, baseball, and other modern sports preoccupy the Hawaiians.

The season of leisure and sport in old Hawaii was the holiday festival called makahiki, which lasted from about mid-October until the end of February. The Hawaiians were taxed annually by their chiefs. At the end of this process of gathering what was due and when crops were harvested, there was the well-earned opportunity for relaxation while intertribal war was prohibited. The working year was arduous, so this season of fun and sport was entered into with enthusiasm.

Competitive sports, such as canoe racing, surfing, sledding, and swimming, were well organized. Stone discs or darts of wood were aimed between small posts set in the earth, checkers were played with black and white pebbles on boards of wood or stone, and other games were enjoyed. The gambling urge was very strong among the old-time Hawaiians. Men occasionally staked wives, canoes, and other possessions on luck. One game was that of guessing under which of several barkcloth bundles a stone had been placed. Cockfighting, stilt walking, wrestling, somersaulting, top spinning, and other pastimes were entered into with hilarity. After the makahiki season the populace returned to hard work and survival by watchfulness and warfare.

STRENUOUS SPORTS and PASSIVE PASTIMES
PAHE'E • THE SLIDING DART
THE PAHE'E: MADE OF WOOD AND HIGHLY POLISHED; VARIED IN LENGTH FROM 2 TO 5 FEET
ULU MAIKA • BOWLING
PUHENEHENE • HIDE THE STONE
RAY LANTERMAN

# 23 Beverages of Kava and Coffee

THE EARLY HAWAIIANS HAD TWO BEVERAGES: WATER AND 'awa which is widely known by its South Pacific name of 'kava.' Kava was made by crushing the dried root of the pepper plant, *Piper methysticum*. Girls and boys chewed the root, spat the masticated mass into a bowl, then added water. Fibrous matter was then strained out, leaving a brownish liquid which was served in coconut cups either as a regular drink or with ritual observance.

The narcotic property of kava relaxed men after their toils. Chiefs and priests used it during their social gatherings and in their rituals. Dried kava roots were appropriate offerings to the gods. Overindulgence in kava caused the skin to scale, the eyes to become bloodshot, and the body to tremble.

Coffee has replaced 'awa as Hawaii's favorite non-alcoholic drink. Coffee production is an important industry on the Kona Coast of the Big Island, where volcanic soil, rainfall, and climate are ideal for cultivation. Farms range along the coastal slopes of Mauna Loa between the 500- and 3,000-foot levels. Kona coffee is strong and bitter, much appreciated by connoisseurs. However, most of the Kona crop is sold abroad for use in coffee blends.

The coffee shrub or tree originated in Arabia, Ethiopia, and Abyssinia, then spread through tropical lands. An enterprising gardener, Don Marin, first introduced the coffee plant to Hawaii in 1817. In 1825 John Wilkinson, gardener to O'ahu's Governor Boki, planted Brazilian seedlings in Manoa Valley. So began Hawaii's coffee industry.

THE AWA CEREMONY
ROOT AND LEAF OF THE KAVA
AFTER FEHER
... A LITTLE DIFFERENT FROM TODAY'S COFFEE BREAK
COFFEE TREE
RAY LANTERMAN

# 24 Hawaii's Sacred Red-Flowered Tree

THE HAWAIIAN TREE CALLED 'OHI'A LEHUA USUALLY HAS its wood referred to as 'ohi'a and its flower lehua. This tree has a special place in Hawaiian lore as being associated with the volcano goddess Pele and her younger sister, Hi'iaka.

It is usually found on Hawaii's islands at elevations from 1,000 to 9,000 feet. Forests of the tree exist on Hawaii and Kaua'i in form from shrubs to giants. In season, it puts forth flaming red blossoms. The trunks are typically knarled. The wood is hard and durable and of a reddish colour that, along with the flowers, reinforce its association of the tree with the supernatural, as red is a color sacred to high deities. God images were often made from this wood. It was also a favorite for canoe hulls.

The 'ohi'a lehua often has poetical references in Hawaiian chants and songs, notably to Pele of volcanoes and fire, and her sister, Hi'iaka, who was a guardian of forests of this tree, especially those of Pele's home on the Big Island. To pluck a lehua blossom without due ritual observance of Pele was to invite the anger of the goddess, who is to this day loved and feared by many Hawaiians. One widespread belief is that if one plucks lehua flowers when advancing up mountain trails rain storms will follow. Incidentally, Hawaii law forbids the plucking of these flowers from trees in State parks.

Legend tells that Pele, in a fit of jealous anger when her sister Hi'iaka became affectionate with Pele's lover, the Kaua'i chief Lohiau, destroyed by lava and fire Hi'iaka's sacred groves. To this day volcanic eruptions cause lava flows that continue to consume tracts of 'ohi'a forests. Quite apart from this occasional destruction on western Hawaii where the mountain Mauna Loa is still active, this sacred tree is declining throughout the islands.

# OHIA LEHUA

## A FLASHY FLOWER AND A USEFUL WOOD

# 25 Exotic Flora of the Islands

THE FLORA OF HAWAII HAS THREE DIVISIONS. THERE IS endemic flora usually limited to specific regions, such as the silversword which grows only on Maui. There are indigenous plants and trees native not only to Hawaii but to wider Pacific regions, such as the breadfruit tree which is found on many Polynesian islands. Thirdly, there are the exotic or introduced plants and trees of post-European times.

The more than two thousand endemic plants are little known and rarely seen by visitors. They are usually inconspicuous and are 'native' in the sense they were not introduced by the early Polynesian settlers of these islands who brought only useful food plants.

In the urban areas, in hotel and private gardens and the streets of towns and country are numerous imported plants and trees. They are more conspicuous than the endemic and introduced native plants. The brilliantly colored hibiscus is a newcomer that obscures the small white hibiscus native to Hawaii. The Mexican cactus, or night-blooming cereus, which flourishes along the walls of Punahou School, came from Mexico. The angel's trumpet is from India; the flame tree belongs to Madagascar; jacaranda is native to Brazil. The ironwood and eucalyptus are from Australia, and the bo tree is from Ceylon. And so the catalog continues.

Exotic blossoms of flamboyance spring from imported shrubs or trees. The plumeria, also known as frangipani, is from Southeast Asia; gardenia (China); allamanda and bougainvillea (Brazil); oleander (Asia Minor); pussy tail (East Indies); jasmine and jade vine (Philippines); tiare (Society Islands) and giant orchid (Malaysia). All are the delight of botanists and make life in Hawaii just so more colorful.

HAWAII'S FLORA EXOTICA
NIGHT-BLOOMING CEREUS: SHOWY FLOWERS FROM JUNE TO OCTOBER
BIRD OF PARADISE
ANTHURIUM
... AND ORCHIDS GALORE
SILVERSWORD BLOOMS IN THE RAREFIED ATMOSPHERE HIGH IN THE CRATER OF HALEAKALA
RAY LANTERMAN

# 26 Saga of the Sugar Industry

PRIOR TO THE ARRIVAL OF EUROPEANS THE HAWAIIANS lived in a well-balanced subsistence economy. Changes were few and slow. The arrival of Europeans brought rapid change. Money was introduced, along with ideas of trade. The salt and sandalwood industries and the provisioning of ships with hogs, water, and firewood steadily established a money economy in Hawaii. The most devastating effect on Hawaiian life came in the latter half of the 19th century when the burgeoning of the sugar industry, after a humble beginning at Koloa, Kaua'i, in 1835, grew as a kind of monster as far as the Hawaiians were concerned. The demands for more and more land, water and labor by the sugar planters was foreign to Hawaiian ways of thinking and furthermore they could see no point in sweating under the hot sun in dusty cane fields. The planters brought in foreign labor to work the crops and the Hawaiians soon became a minority in their own land.

The rise of the great sugar companies, into whose hands much of the wealth of the realm accumulated, created a European elite who not only dominated polite society of the time but, to a great extent, controlled government. Sugar transformed Hawaii.

The first solid demand on sugar and other food exports occurred in the 1840's to meet the needs created by the California gold rush. The American Civil War of 1861-65 which devastated the southern states brought about new industries, also the American march westward begun. The demand for Hawaiian sugar increased with each passing decade. This boom continued until World War II, however the rise of foreign competition from lands where labor was cheap and land plentiful brought about instability of price obtainable for Hawaiian sugar. From the 1970's sugar production has declined and those plantations still in operation are, in the 1980's, in financial trouble. Furthermore, tourism has replaced sugar as Hawaii's number one industry. It appears that by the end of the 20th century sugar cane fields will diminish to the point of being a curiosity.

TALL, SWEET GRASS
A VERY EARLY SUGAR MILL: JUICE WAS EXTRACTED BY CRUSHING THE CANE BETWEEN STONE GRINDERS POWERED BY A WALKING CARIBAO
TODAY, HAWAII'S MILLS PRODUCE OVER A MILLION TONS OF RAW SUGAR A YEAR, WHICH IS STORED IN HUGE SHEDS TO AWAIT BULK-SHIPMENT TO THE REFINERY IN THE HOLDS OF "SUGAR TANKERS"
RAY LANTERMAN

# 27 The Pineapple in Hawaii's History

PINEAPPLE, NICKNAMED THE "QUEEN OF FRUITS," IS AS representative of the Hawaiian Islands as hula girls. The Hawaiians called it "hala kahiki" because it resembles the fruit of the native hala tree, yet is foreign ("kahiki" means a distant foreign place). Older residents refer to the pineapple as "King Pine," knowing it was once second only to sugar in the Hawaiian economy.

The pineapple is said to be of Brazilian origin. It was introduced to Hawaii in 1813 by a botanist, Don Francisco de Paula y Marin, an advisor to Kamehameha the Great. Marin notes in his diary for January that year: "This day I planted pineapples."

The first commercial pineapple plantings were at Kailua-Kona on Hawaii's Big Island where the fruit was traded to whaling ships. Later it was exported to booming California. However, the quick ripening of the fruit made this an unprofitable business fraught with uncertainty.

In 1899, a young New Englander, James D. Dole, established pineapple lands at Wahiawa on O'ahu and in time he created the modern industry of canning pineapple. In post-World War II years the high cost of land and labor in Hawaii and foreign competition caused the pineapple industry to decline. In the 1980's it is heading for extinction as a major industry along with sugar production. No doubt pineapple will be grown commercially in Hawaii for decades to come as the picturesque "pine" is appreciated by tourists who not only enjoy the fresh fruit eaten in Hawaii but as a novelty to send or carry back home.

COLUMBUS
JUST COULDN'T
SEEM TO STOP
DISCOVERING
THINGS—
ANANAS COMOSUS,
FOR EXAMPLE
RAY
LANTERMAN

# 28 Luscious Fruits from Far Lands

Visitors to Hawaii delight not only in Hawaii's sunny beaches where coconut palms wave before the tradewinds. They also enjoy the remarkable range of luscious tropical fruits grown in the islands. Pre-European Hawaii was generally arid over much of its land. Juicy fruits were lacking. The Hawaiians had the coconut with its flesh and milk, bananas, breadfruit, the mountain apple, and some edible berries. However, the introduced fruit trees of Hawaii of today were unknown. Valleys and plains that were a century ago dry lands now yield exotic fruit crops such as avocado, guava, mango, limes, and oranges. The introduction of hundreds of kinds of fruits, coupled with exploitation of subterranean water resources, has made Hawaii a gardener's paradise.

All the subtropic and tropic worlds of the earth have contributed to this now fruitful place. Avocado of three kinds are from West India, Guatemala, and Mexico; the turkey fig is from the Middle East; the lychee from China; the mulberry from Iran; the persimmon from Asia. Fruits with strange names are here to be found: the tamarind, sweetsop, soursop, pummelo, star-apple, loquat, cherimoya, carambola, carrisa, and acerola, to name a few. Hawaii is indeed a fruit lover's paradise.

Hawaiian production cannot meet the needs of the market and in these days of airfreight services perishable fruits, such as the "kiwi fruit" of New Zealand, are flown from thousands of miles away. There is one summer fruit that is so abundant it is left to rot in gardens and on roadways — it is the delicious mango which is, in its way, *the* fruit tree of Hawaii today.

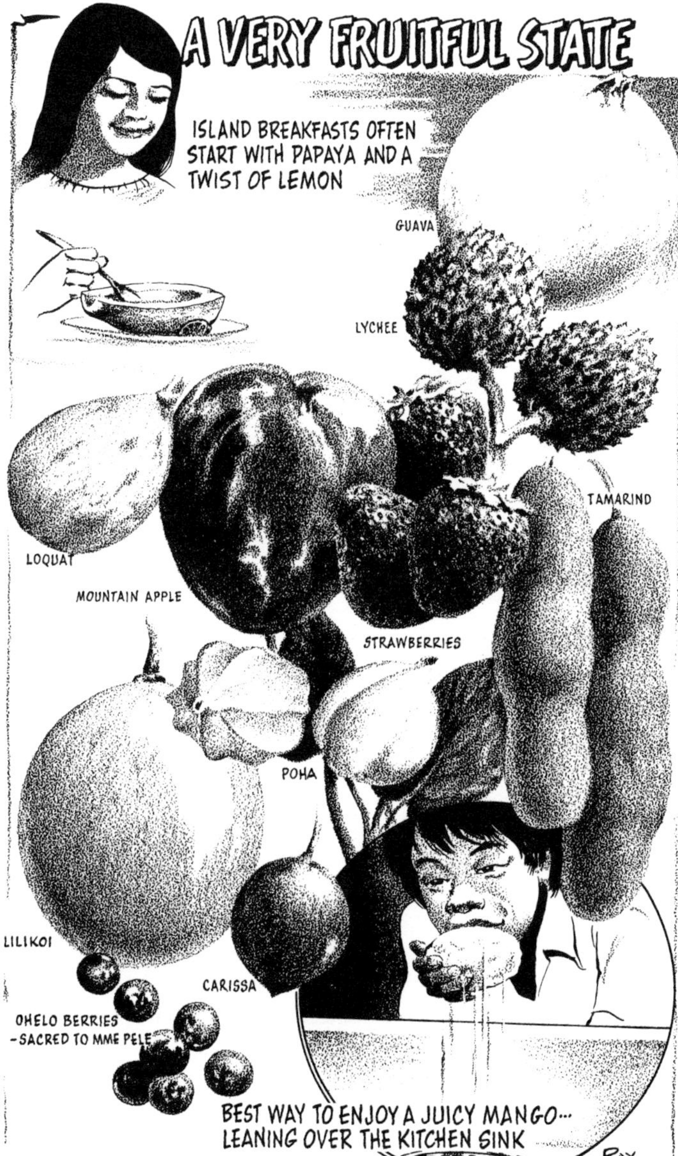
A VERY FRUITFUL STATE
ISLAND BREAKFASTS OFTEN START WITH PAPAYA AND A TWIST OF LEMON
GUAVA
LYCHEE
TAMARIND
LOQUAT
MOUNTAIN APPLE
STRAWBERRIES
POHA
LILIKOI
CARISSA
OHELO BERRIES -SACRED TO MME PELE
BEST WAY TO ENJOY A JUICY MANGO... LEANING OVER THE KITCHEN SINK
RAY LANTERMAN
ALL EXCEPT PAPAYA AND MANGO SHOWN 1/2 SIZE

# 29 Salt in Old Hawaii

HAWAIIANS NEEDED, ALONG WITH ALL MANKIND, A SUPPLY of that most important mineral, sodium chloride, known to most of us as salt. They required it for health and tastebud satisfaction. Their method of making salt was to leave seawater to evaporate in stone pans or clay-lined pools under the hot summer sun. The coarse salt crystals so produced were ground to powder with stone pestle and mortar.

Hawaiian salt is in its most typical form of a reddish-brown color from the ochreous earth used to line evaporating pools. This added mineral gives to this salt a particular tang that connoisseurs say exactly compliments Hawaiian foods. A small amount of salt supply was gathered from depressions in coastal rocks over which spray had thrown sea water where it evaporated.

The Hawaiians also manufactured a fine white salt. Captain Cook and later ships' captains found local salt excellent for preserving pork provisions. The salt of the Kealakekua Bay region was described by Lieutenant King as being "white and of most excellent quality and abundance."

In the days before refrigeration salt was used as the primary food preservative. An important salt industry grew up in Hawaii in the 19th century, notably to meet the needs of passing ships. It was exported to California for the hide industry and to Russian Alaska for fish salting. The production of salt continues on a small scale in Hawaii at Hanapepe on Kaua'i where certain families hold rights to work the ponds. Visitors to Kaua'i may visit these ponds but it is only at certain times that they can see people working them.

# Sun, Sea, and SALT

FROM A CATCHMENT BASIN AT THE SHORE, SEA WATER WAS LET INTO SHALLOW RECTANGULAR SALT PANS *(KAHEKA)* WHERE EVAPORATION PRODUCED SALT.

FOR HOUSEHOLD USE, SEA WATER WAS EVAPORATED IN STONE DISHES CALLED *POHO KAHAPAʻAKAI*: THE COARSE CRYSTALS WERE THEN GROUND FINE WITH A STONE MULLER

# 30 Cash Cargoes of Sandalwood

THE SANDALWOOD TREE WHICH ONCE GREW IN ABUNDANCE in early Hawaii from about 1800 to the 1830's became both a blessing and a curse. For a time, export of sandalwood was Hawaii's major source of cash income until, with the depletion of trees, the industry ended.

A story is told that a ship's captain who had collected firewood on the island of Kaua'i one evening sniffed the fragrance of sandalwood with which he had become familiar when in Chinese ports. It immediately dawned on him he had discovered a woody gold mine. So began a trade from which enormous fortunes were made.

When cargoes of sandalwood reached China, the Hawaiian Islands became known to the Chinese as "Tan Heong Shan," that is, "The Sandalwood Mountains." The wood sold in Canton for about nine dollars a pical, about 133 pounds.

King Kamehameha was quick to grasp the value of the sandalwood trade. He reserved it to himself and received from it the first large cash income ever known in Hawaii. He put Hawaiian villagers to work gathering trees from the mountains. Their loads were placed in pits dug in the earth, roughly shaped in the form of a ship's hold. This allowed estimated cargo quantities. Kamahameha exchanged such accumulated cargoes for dollars or ships.

At his death in 1819 his son, Liholiho, bowed to the pressure of chiefs who wanted a share in the wealth of the sandalwood trade which Kamehameha had never allowed to go beyond his personal control. Unfortunately greedy chiefs regarded this permission as a license to exploit the common people. Men, women, and children were hounded like slaves into the uplands to harvest sandalwood. Their food, clothing, and shelter was inadequate while the labor was heavy. Many weakened and died. When all accessible trees were harvested the trade ended. Fishing and farming, the traditional occupations of Hawaiians had been neglected due to this enforced absence from the villages. The result was the Hawaiian basic economy was disrupted.

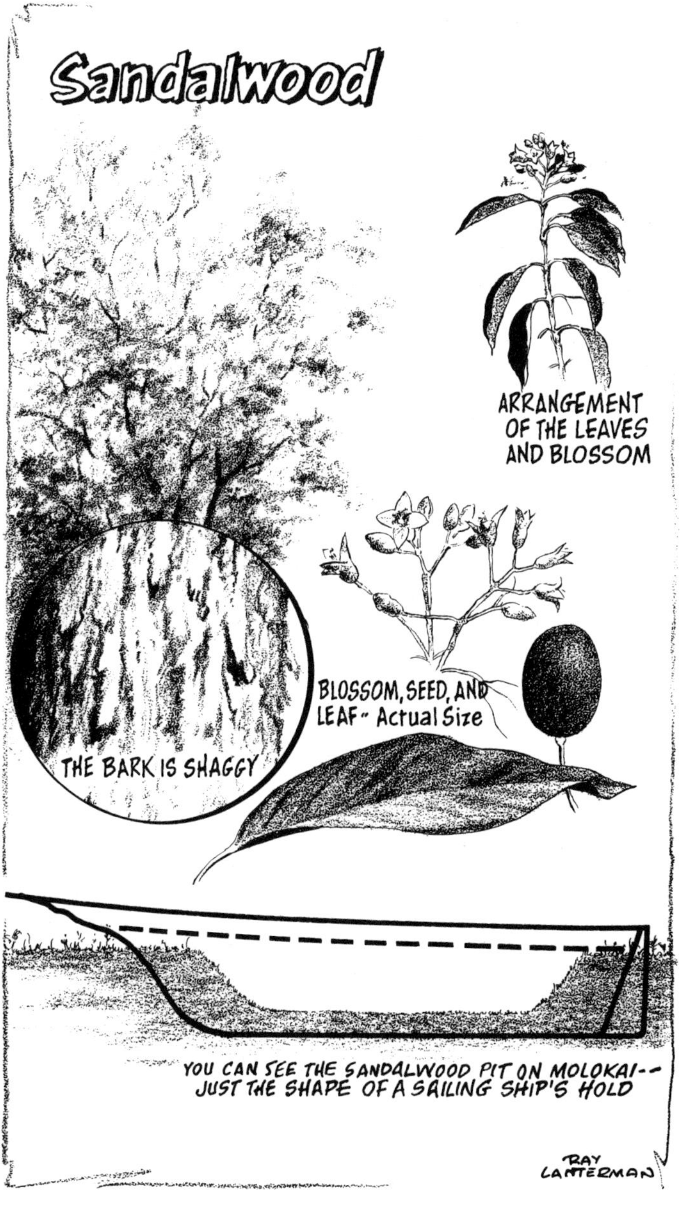
Sandalwood
ARRANGEMENT OF THE LEAVES AND BLOSSOM
BLOSSOM, SEED, AND LEAF -- Actual Size
THE BARK IS SHAGGY
YOU CAN SEE THE SANDALWOOD PIT ON MOLOKAI-- JUST THE SHAPE OF A SAILING SHIP'S HOLD
RAY LANTERMAN

# 31 Whaling in Hawaii

THE ROMANTIC STORY OF WHALING IN HAWAII IS CENTERED on the old Hawaii capitol of Lahaina, Maui. At the height of the whaling industry several hundred ships would anchor there for refreshment and refit, awaiting the summer season of Arctic seas. Honolulu was the second center of catering to whalers.

The first European mariners to reach Hawaii were from exploring expeditions of Britain, France, and Russia. Captain James Cook was the first to land in Hawaii, on Kauai, in 1778. These early visitors reported the abundance of whales in the Pacific at a time when the numbers of Atlantic whales were declining to depletion. Consequently, it was not long before Atlantic whaling ships ventured into the Pacific via Cape Horn. In 1819 the New Bedford whalers, *Balen* and *Equator*, visited Hawaii. Then rich whaling grounds were found off Japan, and swarms of vessels came to reap new whale harvests. The Hawaiian Islands or Sandwich Islands as they were then called, offered an ideal place for ships to refit, reprovision and recreate their crews. Lahaina on Maui offered sheltered anchorages, provisioning and refit services as well as grog shops and girls. It was an unwritten law among whalemen that once around Cape Horn they were free to do as they wished.

On the positive side, whaling fleets brought a wealth of dollars and goods paid in return for wood, water, hogs, root crops, and other items. This trade replaced the recently lost revenue of the depleted sandalwood trade. The volume of business is indicated by the 596 ships that came to the Islands in 1846. The discovery of petroleum in America in 1859 and the attacks on whale ships by Confederate naval forces in the Civil War of the 1860's dealt a severe blow to the whaling industry. Mineral oil from American soil deflated the price of whale oil. The final blow which virtually ended Pacific whaling as a highly profitable industry was the destruction of whaling fleets in 1871 and 1876 when early ice freezes in Arctic waters captured and crushed many ships.

"NANTUCKET SLEIGH RIDE"
A HARPOONED WHALE RACES OFF, TOWING THE WHALE BOAT AT A FAST CLIP. WHEN THE WHALE WEAKENS THE BOAT WILL PULL ALONGSIDE AND THE MATE WILL THRUST A RAZOR-SHARP LANCE INTO THE ANIMAL FOR THE KILL.

FROM A DRAWING BY TABER, CA. 1870

# 32 The Hawaiian Youth Who Inspired Missionaries

THE DEVASTATING EFFECTS OF INTRODUCED DISEASES, the technical superiority of European civilization, and the coming of a new religion and social order caused the successor of Kamehameha the Great, his son Liholiho, to declare the traditional Polynesian religion of Hawaii was defunct. In 1819 he ordered that temples and god images be destroyed. The path to the Christianization of Hawaii was relatively easy as the first missionary party that arrived from New England in 1820 found a devout people without a religious faith.

The pioneer missionary group that braved the stormy Atlantic and forbidding Cape Horn was inspired in its endeavors by a Hawaiian youth who, born in 1792, had shipped on a whaler in 1809. Somehow, he found his way to Andover Theological Seminary, Massachusetts, where he pleaded for teachers to be sent to enlighten his people whom he described as living savage lives.

This young man, named Opukaha'ia, a word meaning 'stomach cut open,' suggesting he was born by Cesarean section, was given the Christian name of Henry. He told how, at the age of ten years, he had seen his parents and younger brother killed in a tribal battle. Disgusted with the bloodthirstiness of his countrymen, he determined to seek for them more civilized manners.

His pleas did not fall on deaf ears for at that time all of Europe and America were looking for people to convert to Christianity and the Bible. Opukaha'ia was enrolled in a foreign mission school in Cornwall, Connecticut, along with some other Hawaiian youths in order to prepare them to return to Hawaii as native missionaries. For Opukaha'ia this happy return was not to be, as he died of typhus, February 1818, at the age of 26 years.

THIS YOUNG MAN'S URGENT PLEA CHANGED THE COURSE OF HAWAII'S HISTORY
HENRY OPUKAHA'IA
RAY LANTERMAN

# 33 Hawaii's First Missionaries

THE CONGREGATIONAL MISSIONARIES WHO REACHED HAWAII in 1820 were hardy men and women. Their ship was the 85-foot brig *Thaddeus*, a vessel cramped and uncomfortable. This was Hawaii's "Mayflower," as the descendants of this first missionary company became a kind of social elite whose names, ring out to this day.

Also aboard were four youths described as "Hawaiian helpers from Cornwall School." As they are more or less forgotten, let us recall their names here. They were Thomas Hopu, William Kanui, John Honoli'i and George Kaumuali'i, son of the king of Kaua'i. In all, twelve missionary "companies" came to Hawaii, the last in 1848.

The success of the missionaries in converting the Hawaiians was so rapid that the New England authorities decided that Hawaii's missions were quite able to support themselves. Primary financial aid was reduced or cut off. The result was that many missionaries, and certainly the majority of their descendants, turned to commerce and the acquisition of land. The children of mission families became powerful, and in control of much of the wealth, dictated policy even to Hawaii's kings.

Who can blame them that they made the best of opportunity? Some say that as the Hawaiians prayed to heaven, looking upwards, the missionaries, with Bible in one hand, grabbed lands with the other hand. That some did is true, yet most of them worked hard to civilize a wild place. They put the Hawaiian language in print, they taught reading, writing, and arithmetic and practical skills of the western world. Let us be tolerant of them and admire their many achievements. They left an indelible stamp on Hawaiian society, built many beautiful churches and associated buildings.

THE HAWAIIANS WERE SUSPICIOUS WHEN THE MISSIONARIES DUG THE FIRST CELLAR THEY'D EVER SEEN...
They're up to something— What do you suppose they're going to hide down there?
THAT CELLAR IS STILL THERE. YOU CAN WALK THROUGH A SWINGING GATE AND VISIT THE MISSION HOUSES IN THEIR CHARMING SETTING ON KING STREET NEAR HONOLULU'S CITY HALL
PRE-FAB FRAME HOUSE
ADOBE BUILDING
OTHER EARLY MISSIONARY STRUCTURES, AND STILL IN USE:
"OLD SCHOOL HALL," PUNAHOU SCHOOL CAMPUS WAS BUILT IN 1852
RAY LANTERMAN
KAULANAPUEO CHURCH · HUELO, MAUI

# 34 Westminster Abbey of Coral

When Christianity came to Hawaii in 1820 the need arose for churches, schools, and homes for the missionaries. The earliest structures were only frames with thatched roofs. In time, wherever a mission was established, a variety of buildings appeared, some being more substantial than others. The Protestant missionaries of New England, and later the Catholics, were all intent on making more churches and improving those that existed. Many such buildings are still used as places of Christian worship.

The most spectacular of the early churches is Kawaiaha'o, situated in Honolulu's historic district. This building is often referred to as "Hawaii's Westminster Abbey." Kawaiaha'o's cornerstone was laid in 1839, then built from about 14,000 coral blocks quarried from the shore reef. Before land reclamation, the sea was only a few hundred feet away. The reigning monarch of the time, Kamehameha III, named Kauikeaouli, organized communal effort to make the building and he appointed the Governor of Oahu, Kekuanao'a, to head the project. The Reverend Hiram Bingham, the dominant member of the first New England missionary party, designed the structure and acted as supervisor in general.

Today, Kawaiaha'o stands in all its glory not far from Iolani Palace and adjacent to the various missionary buildings. The graveyard in its grounds is one of Hawaii's most historic cemeteries. Each Sunday services are held in an atmosphere of old Hawaii. Visitors inclined to the historic and religious observance should not miss a Sunday service at Kawaiha'o. The royal pew still stands within. Here indeed is a home place of Christianity in Hawaii.

Kawaiahao
THE ROYAL PEW

# 35 Strange Cargoes to Far Places

THE HISTORY OF HAWAIIAN COMMERCE IS ONE OF UNUSUAL cargoes. The *Sandwich Island Gazette* of 1836 listed export merchandise as cattle hides, goat skins, salt, arrow root, bark cloth, tobacco, firewood, beans, timber, cotton, molasses, coffee, indigo dye, sweetmeats, Indian corn, kukui nut oil for paints, beef, pork, leather, the "pulu" moss for mattress stuffing, sandalwood, red ochre, and other products. Sugar, pineapples, coconut oil, and other goods were later added to this assorted list.

The most unusual of small cargoes were bundles of soiled fine linen and lace that some European residents sent to San Francisco to Chinese laundries for careful washing, starching, and ironing.

Old-time transportation of goods in Hawaii was by men or women walking, using carrying poles with bundles hanging from each end, or by small cargoes taken on board single or double canoes. With the coming of Western sailing ships interisland and foreign freight became modernized. Canoes gave way to sailing ships then steamships arrived, followed by motor vessels.

Harbors in Hawaii were rarely accessible to ships due to reefs and sand bars. Sheltered waters, such as at Honolulu, Lahaina, and Kealakekua Bay, offered safe anchorages that served well enough. Most cargoes were taken on in open coastal roadsteads. Today, air transportation of goods, freight barges and great container ships entering developed harbors have resolved Hawaii's cargo problems.

"—AND TELL THEM TO USE MORE STARCH IN YOUR COLLARS THIS TIME—"
RAY LANTERMAN

# 36 Hawaii's Many Religious Faiths

HAWAII'S MANY-CULTURED SOCIETY HAS VARIOUS RELIGIOUS faiths. Hawaii's relatively small population of about one million, and a visitor count of five million annually (in mid-1980s) suggests that every religious belief in the world is in some way represented in this State. This multi-religious, multi-racial, and multi-ethnical Hawaiian society has an in-built religious tolerance. Catholic priests and Protestant clergymen mix on equal terms with Buddhists and gurus from India and Tibet. The first faith of Hawaii was that of the Polynesians. This religion served these islands for a thousand years.

By 1819 the impact of visiting Europeans with their new ideas of heaven and earth, was such that King Kamehameha II decided that the old gods be abandoned and the temples burnt. The New England Protestant missionaries arrived in 1820 to find a religious vacuum, and it was not long before Christianity was the religion of the land.

Today, Hawaii has everything in the way of religious faiths and a fine array of churches, temples, and synagogues. The ancient Hawaiian temples remain as revered piles of stone which have become tourist attractions.

The illustration shows the "Praying Hands" of the German artist Dürer and, clockwise, the Christian cross, the wheel of Buddhism, a god image of Hawaii, the arch of Islam, the Hindu symbol "Om" – the name of God, a Japanese Shinto gate, the yin-yang circle of Chinese Taoism, and the Jewish Star of David.

CLOCKWISE FROM TOP: CHRISTIANITY, BUDDHISM, ANCIENT HAWAIIAN, ISLAMIC, HINDUISM, SHINTOISM, TAOISM, JUDAISM

# 37 Father Damien, the Good Shepherd of Moloka'i

FATHER DAMIEN, THE ROMAN CATHOLIC PRIEST FAMOUS for devoting his life to the leper patients of Kalaupapa on the island of Moloka'i, is among Hawaii's heroes. He was selected, along with King Kamehameha the Great to represent Hawaii in the statuary Hall of Fame in Washington, D.C.

The bronze image of Father Damien standing before the State Capitol in Honolulu is an angular figure depicting Damien with priest's hat, cane, and eye glasses on a face disfigured by leprosy. This sculpture, because of its modernism, caused great controversy when it was first presented by the Venezuelean sculptress Marisole Escobar. The sculpture of the illustration here is a conventional carrara marble version created by the Belgium artist Maurice Felbier showing Father Damien helping a leper patient to rise. This now stands in the Holy Rosary Church, Upper Paia, Maui.

Father Damien, named Joseph Damien De Veuster, was born at Tremeloo, Belgium, in 1840. At twenty years of age he entered the Congregation of Sacred Hearts and was soon after sent to Hawaii as a missionary in 1864. For nine years he labored among the Hawaiians in apostolic work, building churches and tending the sick and needy. About this time an epidemic of leprosy, believed introduced by Chinese immigrants, broke out. It was called by the Hawaiians "ma'i pake," which means "the Chinese sickness." Damien devoted himself to leprosy victims, and in 1889 he died one of them. Today leprosy is treatable. Patients are free to live normal lives and need not suffer the terribly disfiguring symptoms that made the disease so feared in Damien's time.

ME KE ALOHA POINA OLE

WARMEST LOVE NOT FORGOTTEN

DAMIEN: STATUE AT HOLY ROSARY CHURCH, PAIA, MAUI

RAY LANTERMAN

# 38 The World's Largest "Christmas Tree"

VISITORS TO HAWAII ARE OFTEN IMPRESSED BY THE TALL AND symmetrical pine trees that look like giant Christmas trees. The islands of Kaua'i and Lana'i have large numbers of such trees, however they are to be seen on all islands.

People ask, "Where did they come from?" because they seem so foreign to Hawaii's vegetation. These trees are from the South Pacific. Most look alike to visitors yet they are two distinctive trees. One is the "Cook Pine" (*Araucaria columnaris*) named after Captain James Cook who came across them on an island of New Caledonia which he named "The Island of Pines." The second pine is from Norfolk Island, a mere speck of land discovered by Captain Cook in 1774, called by botanists *Araucaria heterophylla*.

Both pines have cone-yielding seeds that can be easily carried, planted, and cultivated. They are useful in Hawaii as wind breaks and as ornamental trees. As they cross-fertilize, hybrids exist and it is difficult to always say with certainty which is a Norfolk and which a "Cook Pine." The pure Norfolk Pine is symmetrical while the Cook Pine tends to have a less straight trunk and branches that do not always match the idea of a Christmas tree.

Trees growing in places subject to the pressure of the northeast trade winds tend to grow at a slanting angle away from the wind. Those that are in sheltered places or in forests of the tree, such as on Lana'i, rise up as stately spires. The Cook and Norfolk pines are certainly noble and are among the most impressive of Hawaii's foreign trees.

# Hawaii's own Christmas Tree

# 39 The First King to Circumnavigate the World

DAVID KALAKAUA, WHO BECAME HAWAII'S MOST IMAGINATIVE king, was born in Honolulu in 1836. He was also the first Hawaiian monarch not in the hereditary line of Kamehameha the Great. His sister Liliuokalani was destined, by sad fate, to be the last ruling monarch of the Hawaiian kingdom, overthrown by foreign residents in 1893.

Kalakaua was a romantic man with a deep interest in ancient lore had a burning ambition to restore the best of old Hawaii. For example it is largely due to him that the Hawaiian dance of hula survived as both an art and a means of transmitting traditional culture. That Kalakaua drank too much, gambled, and lived a fast life, need not concern us here. He was a man of vision in difficult times. He died in San Francisco in 1891 where he had gone for medical treatment, much lamented by his subjects.

Kalakaua did many unusual things. In 1881 he set out on a tour of the world to seek foreign immigrant labor and to learn how his fellow kings and queens lived. Thus he became the first king to circumnavigate the world. His companions of the voyage were his valet, Robert, who was a fallen nobleman, Chamberlain Charles H. Judd, and the cabinet minister, William Armstrong.

Hawaii was, in the late 19th century, of great strategic interest to Asian and Western nations. Everywhere Kalakaua traveled he was welcomed as a monarch and by his impressive Polynesian stature, excellent English and charm of manner won friends everywhere. He was well received in Japan, France, Russia, Britain, China, India, Egypt, Italy, Belgium, Austria, and Portugal. Today the principal monument to his memory is Iolani Palace, which he built. Completed in 1883, this is the only royal palace in the USA.

# DAVID KALAKAUA

FIRST REIGNING MONARCH TO CIRCUMNAVIGATE THE EARTH

# 40 Postal Services of the Hawaiian Kingdom

WHEN THE HAWAIIAN ISLANDS WERE FOUND BY CHANCE as Captain James Cook traversed the North Pacific in 1779, a world postal system was unknown. The Hawaiians of that time relied for communication on foot runners and canoeists. However, a new age was dawning in Europe due to the rise of industrialism and a modern postal system was being born about the time of the arrival to Hawaii of missionaries from New England in 1820. Western life styles came with them along with the habit of writing letters and sending them by any means available. Letters were the means of communication in mission affairs, business and personal contacts. The missionaries resident in Hawaii penned their letters then awaited the arrival of some ship that would eventually reach America's East Coast.

It was not until 1850 that a formal postal service was established in the Hawaiian Islands. Then a treaty was arranged with the USA for the exchange of mails. The first postmaster, Henry Martyn Whitney, was an efficient man who was a printer. He published in unperforated sheets stamps of value of two, five, and thirteen cents. These first Hawaiian stamps, now called "Missionaries" because most of them have been found on letters sent to New England by missionary correspondents, are highly valued. The Hawaiian "Missionary" stamps, which were cut by scissors from a single sheet, are a philatelist's delight and rank with the most valuable stamps in the world. They were a product of the Hawaiian Monarchy government of King Kamehameha III who reigned from 1825 until his death in 1854. Civilization and an efficient postal service go hand in hand, an axiom no more true than in Hawaii.

THIS STAMP WEIGHS IN AT TWO-THOUSANDTHS OF AN OUNCE: CALCULATING AT ITS MARKET VALUE, THE GOSSAMER PAPER –'PELURE'– IT'S PRINTED ON WOULD BE WORTH MORE THAN
ONE BILLION DOLLARS A POUND!
Hawaiian Postage
2
Two Cents
OTHER RARE STAMPS
H.I. & U.S. Postage
13
13 Cents
1852 "MISSIONARY"... NOTE THE "& U.S."
POSTAGE
5
Honolulu
Hawaiian 1¢
FIVE CTS
1853: KAMEHAMEHA III
INTER ISLAND
HAWAIIAN POSTAGE
2
UKU LETA.
2 Cents.
1859 INTER-ISLAND
REMEMBER WHEN AIR MAIL WAS ONLY SEVEN CENTS? FIRST DAY OF ISSUE FOR THIS STATEHOOD COMMEMORATIVE WAS 21 AUGUST, 1959
HAWAII STATEHOOD • 1959
U.S. AIR MAIL
7¢
RAY LANTERMAN

# 41 James Jackson Jarves, The Versatile Genius

THE HAWAIIAN ISLANDS, SITUATED AT THE NORTHERN tip of Polynesia, have a romantic past. Blue ocean, palms waving before the trade winds, brown maidens and open horizons have drawn many literary men to this Pacific realm. Herman Melville, Robert Louis Stevenson, Richard Henry Dana, Samuel Langhorne Clemens known to the world as Mark Twain, and other men of literary distinction of the 19th century came to Hawaii and wrote about life in these islands. In the early 20th century fictional writing and personal reminiscences of Pacific islands became very popular and a new generation of writers made their way to Hawaii. Jack London visited in 1907, then another great writer, Somerset Maugham, stayed in Honolulu in 1916.

One of the most brilliant literary men who came to these islands was James Jackson Jarves. Little is known of his achievements. He was born in Boston in 1818 and in his lifetime became a noted historian, art critic, editor, merchant, and a pioneer sugar planter. In 1840 he founded a weekly newspaper called *The Polynesian*, then in 1843 he published a book, *The History of the Hawaiian or Sandwich Islands*, the first scholarly history of Hawaii. He also wrote the first Hawaiian novel.

James Jackson Jarves left Hawaii in 1848, never to return. His sensitivity to art led him to writing on aesthetics and painting. Among other achievements he "discovered" the so-called Italian primitive painters and formed a fine collection of them at a time when they were neglected as being too naive to be seriously considered. Yale University saw fit to publish in 1951 a biography, *The Two Lives of James Jackson Jarves*.

# JAMES JACKSON JARVES

CAME TO HAWAII FROM BOSTON WHEN HE WAS 18, AND WAS THE FIRST TO WRITE A HISTORY OF THE ISLANDS

JARVES ALSO THREW A FEW SNOWBALLS ON MAUNA KEA ..... AND MANAGED TO SINGE HIS CLOTHING AT A LAVA FLOW

# 42 Fresh and Salt Water — Precious Resources

THE HAWAIIAN ISLANDS ARE FAVORED WITH MANY OF Mother Nature's gifts: "Eternal Summer" climate, cool tradewinds, bright sunlight, and pollution-free skies, including the clean waters of land and seas. Pure fresh water is available to meet the needs of residents, visitors, and agricultural and horticultural industries.

The sea waters of the Hawaiian Islands are constantly refreshed as the North Equatorial Current sweeps by, bringing cleansing currents. Hawaii's seashores and ocean waters are the delight of swimmers, surfers, yachtsmen, fishermen, and those who enjoy the pastime of gazing out to sea. Tourism, which has become Hawaii's number one industry, could not exist without its fresh and salt waters. Fishing industries, too, which have great prospects for development, harvest the ocean. Fresh water prawn farming is another feature of Hawaii's water industries.

Hawaii's freshwater resource is a part of a great natural cycle of the North Pacific. The northeast tradewinds bring in moisture-laden air that forms into clouds, then precipitate as rain when they are pushed up into colder mountain air. Much of the rain runs off as groundwater, evaporates, or is taken in by vegetation. Large amounts of water seep through the porous volcanic mountains to form reservoirs that remain as "lens" both above and below sea level. Because fresh and salt water do not readily mix, and lenses are protected by cap-rock formed from old coral masses and lava, water reserves are maintained within high islands. Artesian wells were dug to tap these reservoirs.

The water needs of Hawaii's resident population, notably on the heavily populated island of O'ahu, military establishments and an ever-growing tourism with its highrise hotels has in the 1980's put a strain on the natural water resources of O'ahu, Maui and Hawaii. The extended drought of 1984 required strict water conservation and was a potent of things to come. The sugar industry uses enormous quantities of water.

WATER
WATER
WATER
WATER
WATER
WATER
WATER
WATER
"FUN TO PLAY IN"
BODY SURFING
"FINE FOR YACHT RACING"
"MAKES NICE RAINBOWS"
"FUN TO BUILD CASTLES BY"
WATER
WATER
"AND CANOE RACING"
WATER
WATER
WATER
WATER
WATER
GOOD FOR US FISH, TOO
RAY CANTERMAN
"FUN JUST TO LOOK AT"

# 43 Tsunami and Other Destructive Forces

THE HAWAIIAN ISLANDS ORDINARILY PRESENT A SERENE FACE. Azure seas with waves foaming white over reefs and beaches of golden sand fringed with palm trees bending gently before the tradewinds suggest to visitors that here is paradise. Lurking behind this charming scene is the violence of raw nature, not often seen, yet it is there. Volcanic eruptions, earthquakes, flash floods, hurricanes and tsunami (the Japanese word for 'tidal waves' which waves, incidentally, have nothing to do with tides) vent their destruction from time to time. The advent of some destructive force tends to concentrate on one island or another, or on part of an island, so general devastation does not take place.

Tsunami waves are caused by undersea eruptions, earthquakes local or distant and submarine ridge collapses. The Hawaiian chain is most subject to waves generated by earthquakes on the continental Pacific rim, notably earthquakes of Alaska, California and Chile. As the pressure waves so generated move at about 500 miles an hour modern warning systems allow several hours notice to Hawaii residents when such a tsunami is on the way. The sirens sound and preparations are made for safety. Unfortunately human curiosity causes many to rush to the sea coast to "see the wave come in." Many have drowned because of this urge to witness the event. The front pages of the telephone books for each island provide maps showing areas of possible wave inundation.

The danger of tsunami in Hawaii is not so much from waves originating thousands of miles away as their speed can be estimated and warnings given by radio, sirens and other means. Small local tsunami can be sudden and are often heralded by a earthquake. A wave can mount in seconds. Beach subsidence may also occur such as took the lives of some members of a camping party of a Hawaii bay some years ago. An earthquake or any sudden non-tidal recession of the sea is fair warning of an impending danger from a tsunami. Anyone seeing such a phenomena is advised to move inland, heading for the nearest high land.

TSUNAMI
OMINOUS WARNING
JUST BEFORE THE ARRIVAL OF A TSUNAMI, THE OCEAN RECEDES, EXPOSING FAR-OUT ROCKS AND REEF
RAY LANTERMAN

# 44 Communications Then and Now

COMMUNICATIONS IN OLD-TIME HAWAII WERE SIMPLE. Messengers ran between districts or travelled by canoe. Long-distance signaling was done waving bark cloth or by using the sound of barkcloth wooden beaters hitting on wooden anvils. A kind of Morse code was evolved that enabled women, while at work beating away, to send messages by means of a pulsating sound over valleys and plains. Most communication was by the word of mouth of messengers.

When Europeans settled in Hawaii in the early 19th century, communication by pen and paper improved the situation. Also, Honolulu had a volunteer group of horsemen called "Lookout Charlies" who watched from the heights above the Kaimuki region near Diamond Head for arriving ships. When a vessel appeared the lookout rode in haste to spead the news in Honolulu. Ships carried news in the form of printed papers and letters. In those isolated times everybody was hungry for information from the world beyond the horizon.

The first telephone of Hawaii was that installed by a Mr. Charles H. Dickey of Haiku, Maui. He set up a pair of Graham Bell telephones in 1878 to link his home with his store. Later, King Kalakaua had telephones link Iolani Palace with his boat house where he spent many hours playing poker with cronies. Tradition is that Princess Kaiulani brought these as a gift to him from San Francisco.

In 1880 the Hawaiian Bell Telephone Company was established. The use of telephones grew rapidly. The Mutual Telephone Company in Honolulu established on O'ahu an expanded phone system. This Company became in 1954, the present Hawaiian Telephone Company. Today, undersea cables, transmission via satellites, and other modern devices make interisland and distant communication easy.

# FROM SAIL HO! TO SATELLITE

# 45 Interisland Travel of the Past

BEFORE JET TRAVEL, PASSAGE BETWEEN THE ISLANDS OF Hawaii was made by sea. For centuries Hawaiians used canoes for such journeys, then sailing ships replaced them. In turn, sail was replaced by steamships, then motorships. Interisland passenger services came to an end after World War II. Many long-time residents of Hawaii reminisce on the discomforts of travel on small ships of the early to mid 20th century.

Hawaii's azure seas, clear skies with fluffy white clouds, and gentle tradewinds, suggest that voyages between islands would be a delight. Such trips could be pleasant if sea conditions were good, but the three main dividing seaways had to be crossed to get anywhere. Notorious for choppy waves and strong currents they were a terror to landlubbers. The Kaulakahi Channel separates Kaua'i from O'ahu, the Kaiwi Channel separates Maui from O'ahu. While between Maui and Hawaii is the Alenuihaha Channel. The shores facing these channels are typically rocky and often precipitous. Safe harbors did not originally exist in these regions. Hawaiian canoes could be dragged up on a sandy or rocky beach but deep-keeled ships had no such refuge in bad weather. Sailors and passengers alike just suffered weather conditions as best they could. The 19th century rise of trade and the boom in commercial exports to the West Coast of America, such as salt, sugar, hides, potatoes and dozens of other products was stimulated by conditions brought about by the California gold rush and subsequently the Civil War.

As external trade and interisland commerce developed so did the means of travel between islands and to far places. Now tug-drawn barges handle most inter-island cargoes. Regular sea passenger services do not exist between islands regardless of many attempts to re-establish such facilities.

# ISLAND HOPPING BY SHIP

# 46 Pali Passes of O'ahu

THE ISLAND OF O'AHU, MEANING "GATHERING PLACE," consists of twin volcanoes which joined, forming between them, a high plateau. Trade winds eroded the exposed sides of these islands while the leeward sides are sloping and sheltered. This process of "weathering" has taken millions of years.

When Polynesians settled Hawaii a thousand years ago they had no horses or vehicles. Foot trails and the sea served their simple needs. With Europeans came carts and gigs, then automobiles. Developing commerce and population increases required improved roads.

The main Ko'olau Range, which divides the northern and southern communities of O'ahu, presented a barrier to transportation. Old Hawaiian trails led up Nu'uanu Valley and down the precipitous cliffs of the Pali. (Pali means a cliff). It was a dangerous trail best fitted to barefoot Hawaiians.

In 1854 the Hawaiian Government voted funds to develop a horse carriage road which was completed after many difficulties. The need for a better access to the windward side of O'ahu led to the legislature voting, in 1896, the then enormous sum of $40,000 to build a modern road. John H. Wilson, a young and brilliant engineer, with an associate, Louis Whitehouse, was awarded the contract. In 1897 a labor gang of 250 Hawaiians, Japanese, and Chinese went to work with blasting gunpowder and in time a new road was built.

Progress again demanded quicker access over the range so a tunnel was cut in 1958, then a second tunnel was completed. A second road over the Ko'olau Range called the Likelike Highway with the long Wilson tunnel, was completed in 1961.

When we ride in ease over the two Ko'olau arteries of travel let us not forget the arduous days of foot and horse and the courageous men who made these highways possible.

# THE PALI --IT HASN'T ALWAYS BEEN A BREEZE TO GET FROM HONOLULU TO WINDWARD OAHU

THE PALI "ROAD" IN THE 1800'S. A CARRIAGE *COULD* MAKE IT. RIGHT: AT THE TURN OF THE CENTURY, ENGINEER JOHNNY WILSON BUILT THE FIRST VEHICLE ROAD DOWN THE PRECIPICE. IT HAD 22 SHARP TURNS AND SERVED COMMUTERS FOR NEARLY SIXTY YEARS

TODAY'S PALI AND LIKELIKE HIGHWAYS, WITH THEIR EASY GRADIENTS, SWEEPING CURVES AND TUNNELS, HAVE REDUCED DRIVING TIME BETWEEN WINDWARD AND CENTRAL OAHU TO A MATTER OF MINUTES

SPEAKING OF TUNNELS ~ TO MAUI GOES THE HONOR OF BUILDING THE FIRST CIVILIAN VEHICULAR TUNNEL IN THE ISLANDS, ON HONOAPIILANI HIGHWAY BETWEEN WAILUKU AND LAHAINA. IT WAS OPENED 1 OCTOBER, 1951

# 47 Peter Buck, Dean of Pacific Anthropologists

PETER BUCK WAS BORN IN RURAL TARANAKI AT URANUI, New Zealand, in 1880. His father was an Irishman in the British Constabulary in the New Zealand wars who in times of peace took to farming. Buck's mother, a full-blooded Maori, died when he was a child. He was handed over to a grandmother versed in Maori lore, knowledge which she passed on to an attentive grandson.

This poor country boy was to become a figure of distinction as an authority on the Polynesian peoples, director of the Bernice P. Bishop Museum in Honolulu, and a knighted man of Britain. His life is a remarkable story. Before World War I Buck graduated in medicine at Otago University, Dunedin (New Zealand). Later he served as an officer-soldier in World War I at such ghastly battles as Gallipoli. As a medical doctor he later became a leading advocate of Maori health and hygiene.

As a research scholar and writer of books, Buck published under his Maori name of Te Rangi Hiroa scientific papers and books. His ethnographical studies were published as Bernice P. Bishop Museum bulletins and monographs. To all of his activities he brought to bear the best of both his Maori and European ancestry and left the Pacific world a legacy of new knowledge. When he died in Honolulu in 1951 he was mourned the world over. His ashes were sent to his homeland where they were placed in a memorial vault on a hillside at Okoki, his birthplace, near the town of New Plymouth. In Hawaii he is well loved by those who remember him. The City of Honolulu saw fit to name a street near the Bishop Museum in his memory.

FROM THE SOUTHWESTERN CORNER OF THE POLYNESIAN TRIANGLE CAME
TE RANGI HIROA
PHYSICIAN
STATESMAN
SOLDIER
ANTHROPOLOGIST
DIRECTOR OF THE BERNICE P. BISHOP MUSEUM 1936-1951
A STYLIZED SCULPTURE OF THE PROW OF A MAORI CANOE MARKS SIR PETER'S FINAL RESTING PLACE IN NEW ZEALAND
RAY LANTERMAN

# 48 The Voyaging Canoe Named "Star of Gladness"

SINCE CAPTAIN COOK EXPLORED THE PACIFIC AND discovered many island groups in Polynesia in the later half of the 18th century this question has been debated by scholars: "How did these brown-skinned people find and populate the hundreds of scattered islands as far apart as Hawaii, New Zealand, Easter Island, Tahiti and Marquesas? They had no metal tools or instruments of navigation. Their canoes were capable sailing vessels that could travel long distances but how did they find their way on a trackless sea?" Some scholars said islands were populated by castaway drifters while others insisted that these Polynesians were efficient navigators who used as guides the stars, sun, wind direction, wave patterns, flight of land-based birds and cloud patterns. It has turned out the latter argument is right and this has been demonstrated by the voyages of Hawaii's canoe *Hokule'a* – meaning "Star of Gladness". This name refers to the star Arcturus which passes over Hawaii and so determined for prehistoric voyagers from the South Pacific the latitude of the Hawaiian Islands.

A group called the Polynesian Voyaging Society was formed in Honolulu which built in due time a double-hull sixty foot sailing canoe. Its purpose was to test the theoretical methods of Polynesian non-instrument navigation. This canoe, whose principal designer was the artist-historian Herb Kawainui Kane, was launched at Kualoa Beach Park on O'ahu in the spring of 1975.

In 1976 the *Hokule'a* made a voyage to Tahiti from Hawaii without instruments of navigation. The same feat was repeated in 1980 and in 1985 by the young Hawaiian star navigator Nainoa Thompson aided by the Micronesian Mau Piailug. An epic voyage was headed to New Zealand in 1985.

*Hokule'a* has become a symbol of Hawaiian endeavour and of the "Hawaiian Renaissance" that has over the last decade stirred the Hawaiian people to a new awareness of identity as a distinctive people in a society in which they are a minority.

STARS, SEA, and MAN
RAY
LANTERMAN

# 49 University of Hawaii, A Unique Place of Learning

WHEN THE NEW ENGLAND MISSIONARIES REACHED HAWAII in 1820 they found a charming brown people of high intelligence who lacked a written script. A first objective of the missions was to establish schools, with the Holy Bible, prayer books, and hymnals as standard reading. Translations of such texts into the Hawaiian language proceeded apace after an alphabet was established. The Hawaiians had marvelous memories and were quick to learn to read and write.

In 1842 Punahou School was established on land given by King Kamehameha III to the Reverend Hiram Bingham to build a school suitable for missionary children. It was rechartered as O'ahu College in 1853. Higher education was thus established in Hawaii. This first college was discontinued after a decade but the school continued regular classes.

In 1907 the College of Agricultural and Mechanic Arts became the first public university. It was renamed the College of Hawaii in 1911 with temporary housing at Thomas Square. In 1920 it became the University of Hawaii and has since steadily developed its extensive campus in Manoa Valley. Extension campuses were established in West O'ahu and Hilo to provide university education outside Honolulu. Adjoining the University's Manoa campus is the East-West Center which shares a noble march to knowledge and enlightenment. The University, or "The UH" as it is affectionately called, is a unique institution with a long history of multi-racial and multi-ethnical harmony.

THE YEAR: 1907-08
THE ENROLLMENT: FIVE
THE FACULTY: TWELVE

SO BEGAN

# THE UNIVERSITY OF HAWAII

IN THIS BUILDING NEAR THOMAS SQUARE

John W. Gilmore,
the first President

GROWING IN THE COOL GARDEN COURT OF BACHMAN HALL, THE PRESENT ADMINISTRATION BUILDING, ARE PRITCHARD AND NIUSAWA PALMS — NATIVE TREES OF FIJI — AND A GROUND COVER OF MONDO GRASS (LILY TURF). THE UNIVERSITY'S 124-ACRE *LYON ARBORETUM* EXPERIMENTS WITH 3,000 VARIETIES OF PLANTS FROM ALL PARTS OF THE WORLD.

# 50 Where East and West Do Meet

In Manoa Valley a mile above Waikiki and adjoining the University of Hawaii campus is one of the most noble institutions ever conceived. It is the East West Center which was founded by act of the U.S. Congress in 1960 shortly after Hawaii became a State of America. President Lyndon B. Johnson when a senator pressed for the establishment of this remarkable place. American dollars have never been better spent than in sponsoring the East West Center.

For the first time in history a place has been created in America where students from Asian and Pacific countries are invited to come as undergraduate, graduate and specialist professionals.

This "experiment", if that is what it might be called, has been over a quarter century remarkably successful. The original aim of the East West Center was one of cultural interchange. Adjusting to changing times the focus is now on practicalities, such as technology, economics and population problems of the participant countries. Food production, economical development and such matters have to a great extent given way to abstract scholarly studies.

Grantees and participants of the East West Center programs are privileged people who have unusual opportunities to live the American way of life, study in their respective disciplines, then return to their home countries to apply what they have learnt. The adjacent University of Hawaii, which is an undergraduate, post-graduate and research institution collaborates with its neighbour. Visitors to Hawaii are free to wander about the delightful grounds of both places.

KIPLING RESTATED...

# EAST IS EAST AND WEST IS WEST AND HERE THE TWAIN *DO* MEET

EAST-WEST ROAD IS A BROAD AVENUE THROUGH THE SPACIOUS GROUNDS OF THE EAST-WEST CENTER. IN JEFFERSON HALL (RIGHT) IS A STUDENTS' LOUNGE AND THE "FRIENDS' DESK," WHERE TOURS OF THE GROUNDS MAY BE ARRANGED.

AT LEFT IS THE LANAI OF THE JOHN F. KENNEDY THEATRE

RAY LANTERMAN

# 51 State Capitol of Ineffable Charm

HAWAII HAS A STATE CAPITOL BUILDING THAT IS UNIQUE in the USA. It is an architectural masterpiece set in the heart of Honolulu's historic district. Nearby stands King Kalakaua's coronation rotunda, which is now used by the Royal Hawaiian Band for public concerts, and that monarch's Iolani Palace which is the only royal palace on American soil. On the mountain side of the Capitol is Washington Place, the former home of Hawaii's deposed Queen Liliuokalani and now the Governor's residence. The barracks of the Royal Guard of King Kalakaua are in the palace grounds and adjacent are many places of historic interest.

Within walking distance is Kawaiaha'o Church, a cluster of mission houses open as a museum, and other fascinating places including the State Archives of Hawaii.

The State Capitol was opened on March 15, 1969. Its soaring architecture is impressive and symbolical of all Hawaiian islands. It is here that the life and future of the Hawaiian people is determined. Forty columns represent coconut palms. The conical structures of the House and Senate chambers suggest Hawaii's volcanoes while the pools on both sides indicate the sea which surrounds these delightful islands. The grand central court has an opening to the sky. On the mountain side stands a statue of Father Damien who tended the leper patients of Moloka'i. While on the seaward side is a bronze figure depicting Hawaii's last ruler, Queen Liliuokalani. Massive cast metal replicas of the State Seal hang over both entrances.

ROWS OF PALMS ENCIRCLING TWO MOUNTAINS, AND THE WHOLE SURROUNDED BY WATER: THE UNIQUE SYMBOLISM OF
HAWAII'S STATE CAPITOL
JUST *MAUKA* OF THE CAPITOL, IN A LUSH SETTING OF FERNS AND FLOWERING TREES, IS WASHINGTON PLACE, THE GOVERNOR'S MANSION
RAY LANTERMAN

# 52 Hawaii's Unique Situation

HAWAII WAS ONCE ONE OF THE MOST ISOLATED PLACES on earth set as it is in the middle of the vast North Pacific Ocean. Air travel and fast ships have made it a hub of travel and of military strategy. It is a center of Pacific commerce, tourism and scholarly endeavour. Five million or more tourists annually enjoy its scenic beauty, the fresh ocean airs carried on gentle trade winds and the multiethnical society which lives happily in this Land of Aloha.

Since World War II world attention has moved from the Atlantic to the Pacific. The countries of East Asia, including Japan, and the western seaboard states of the USA have assumed a new role in world affairs. The Hawaiian Islands stand at the center of things in this modern scene and there is little doubt that in time Hawaii shall become widely recognized as America's crucial state in interchange between East and West.

The Hawaiian Island chain reaches over a thousand miles. Of the one hundred and thirty islands, islets, reefs and shoals only Kaua'i, Ni'ihau, O'ahu, Moloka'i, Maui and Hawaii have resident populations. Sea birds, turtles and seals are the only inhabitants of the lonely "outer islands" to the northwest. Incidentally, O'ahu is the hub of the group and it is correct to refer to its adjacent islands as "neighbour islands". The distant uninhabited islands are the "outer islands". It might be added that tourists from the US mainland often use the phrase, "back in the States!" This expression is offensive to local people. Hawaii is a State of the Union with many unique characteristics and a most promising future.

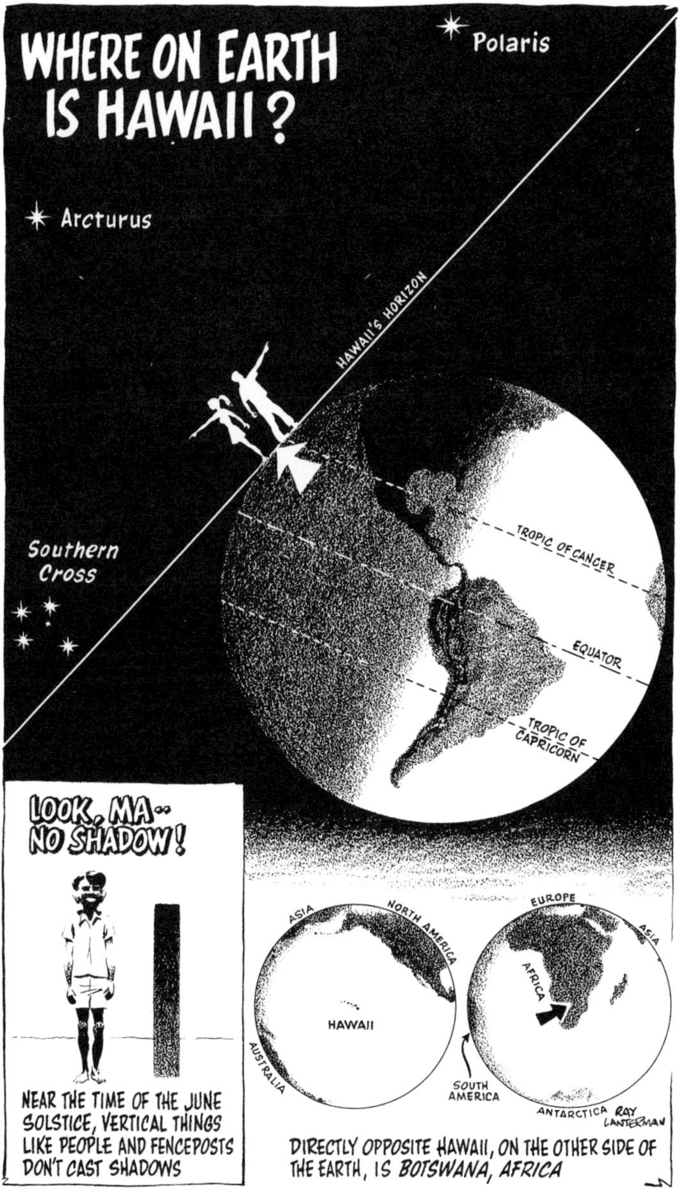
WHERE ON EARTH IS HAWAII?
Polaris
Arcturus
HAWAII'S HORIZON
Southern Cross
TROPIC OF CANCER
EQUATOR
TROPIC OF CAPRICORN
LOOK, MA-- NO SHADOW!
NEAR THE TIME OF THE JUNE SOLSTICE, VERTICAL THINGS LIKE PEOPLE AND FENCEPOSTS DON'T CAST SHADOWS
ASIA
NORTH AMERICA
HAWAII
AUSTRALIA
SOUTH AMERICA
EUROPE
ASIA
AFRICA
ANTARCTICA
RAY LANTERMAN
DIRECTLY OPPOSITE HAWAII, ON THE OTHER SIDE OF THE EARTH, IS *BOTSWANA, AFRICA*

TUTTLE BOOKS ON HAWAII AND THE PACIFIC

**ART AND HANDICRAFTS:**

**Coconut Palm Frond Weaving,** *by William H. Goodloe*

**The New Zealand Maori in Colour,** *by Kenneth & Jean Bigwood and Harry Dansey*

**Tropical Gardening: A Handbook for the Home Gardener,** *by Peggy Hickok Hodge*

**CONCHOLOGY:**

**A Guide to Shell Collecting in the Kwajalein Atoll,** *by Fred B. Borst and Robert D. Coale*

**Handbook for Shell Collectors** (Revised 16th Edition), *by Walter F. Webb*

**1,000 World Sea Shells – Rare to Common: With Values,** *by A. Gordon Melvin and Lorna S. Melvin*

**Pacific Sea Shells,** *by Spencer Wilkie Tinker*

**Sea Shell Parade,** *by A. Gordon Melvin*

**Sea Shells of the World** with Values, *by A. Gordon Melvin*

**Shells of New Guinea and the Central Indo-Pacific,** *by Alan Hinton*

**COOKERY:**

**Hawaiian Cuisine,** *by members of the Hawaii State Society of Washington, D.C.*

**Hawaii Cooks,** *by Maili Yardley*

**HISTORY:**

**An Account of the Polynesian Race:** Its Origin and Migrations, *by Abraham Fornander*

**Ancient Hawaiian Civilization:** A Series of Lectures delivered at the Kamehameha Schools (revised), *by E.S. Craighill Handy and Others*

**Around the World with a King,** *by William N. Armstrong*

**A Complete History of Guam,** *by Paul Carano and Pedro C. Sanchez*

**Dr. Hyde and Mr. Stevenson,** *by H. W. Kent*

**The Drama of Fiji:** A Contemporary History, *by Dr. John Wesley Coulter*

**Guam Past and Present,** *by Charles Beardsley*

**Hawaii: End of the Rainbow,** *by Kazuo Miyamoto*

**The Hawaiians:** An Island People, *by Helen Gay Pratt; drawings by Rosamond S. Morgan and Juliette May Fraser*

**Hawaii's Story by Hawaii's Queen,** *by Liliuokalani*

**Incredible Hawaii,** *by Terence Barrow & Ray Lanterman*

**The Journal of William Ellis,** *by William Ellis*

**Lawrence M. Judd and Hawaii:** An Autobiography, *by Lawrence M. Judd as told to Hugh W. Lytle*

**Okinawa: The History of an Island People,** *by George H. Kerr*

**The Polynesian Family System in Ka-'u Hawai'i,** *by E.S. Craighill Handy and M.K. Pukui*

**Polynesian Researches** (Four Volumes), *by William Ellis*
Vol. 1 – Hawaii
Vol. 2 – Polynesia
Vol. 3 – Society Islands
Vol. 4 – Society, Tubuai Islands & New Zealand

**A Residence of Twenty One Years in the Sandwich Islands,** *by Hiram Bingham*

**Six Months in the Sandwich Islands,** *by Isabella Bird*

**The Voyage of the Flying Bird,** *by Margaret Titcomb*

**LANGUAGE:**

**Dictionary of the Hawaiian Language,** *by Lorrin Andrews*

**An English-Hawaiian Dictionary:** With Various Useful Tables, *by H. R. Hitchcock*

**Hawaiian Phrase Book**

**A Short Synopsis of the Most Essential Points in Hawaiian Grammar,** *by W. D. Alexander*

**LEGENDS AND FOLKLORE:**

**Hawaiian Historical Legends,** *by William D. Westervelt*

**Hawaiian Legends of Ghosts and Ghost-Gods,** *by William D. Westervelt*

**Hawaiian Legends of Old Honolulu,** *by William D. Westervelt*

**Hawaiian Legends of Volcanoes,** *by William D. Westervelt*

**The Legends and Myths of Hawaii:** The Fables and Folk-Lore Of A Strange People, *by His Hawaiian Majesty Kalakaua*

**Myths and Legends of the Polynesians,** *by Johannes E. Andersen*

**Pele and Hiiaka:** A Myth From Hawaii, *by Nathaniel B. Emerson*

**MUSIC AND DANCE:**

**The Unwritten Literature of Hawaii:** The Sacred Songs of the Hula, *collected and translated by Nathaniel B. Emerson*

**NATURAL HISTORY:**

**Australian Crustaceans in Colour,** *by Anthony Healy and John Yaldwyn*

**Australian Insects in Colour,** *by Anthony Healy and C. N. Smithers*

**Australian Seashores in Colour,** *by K. Gillett and J. Yaldwyn*

**Australian Spiders in Colour,** *by Ramon Mascord*

**Birds of Hawaii,** *by George C. Munro*

**Birds in South Vietnam,** *by Philip Wildash*

**Birds of the Southwest Pacific,** *by Ernst Mayr*

**Hawaiian Flowers and Flowering Trees,** *by Loraine E. Kuck & Richard C. Tongg*
(Note: Softcover Edition of this book is entitled, **A Guide to Tropical & Semi-Tropical Flora,** and is also available from Charles E. Tuttle Co.)

**Hawaiian Herbs of Medicinal Value,** *by D. M. Kaaiakamanu and J. K. Akina: translated by Akaiko Akana*

**Pacific Marine Life:** A Survey, *by Charles J. & Diana MacIntyre DeLuca*

**Plant Life of the Pacific World,** *by Dr. Elmer D. Merrill*

**Poisonous Plants of Hawaii,** *by Harry L. Arnold*

**A Portfolio of New Zealand Birds,** *by Bruce Harvey*

**Sharks and Rays,** *by Spencer Wilkie Tinker and Charles J. DeLuca*

**The Shore Fishes of Hawaii,** *by David Starr Jordan & Burton Warren*

**Sport Fishing in Hawaii, Guam & American Samoa,** *by James L. Squire Jr. and Susan E. Smith*

**TRAVEL:**

**Going Native in Hawaii:** A Poor Man's Guide to Paradise, *by Timothy Head*

CHARLES E. TUTTLE COMPANY
PUBLISHERS

28 South Main St. (P.O. Box 410)
Rutland, Vermont 05701-0410 U.S.A.
Suido 1-chome, 2-6, Bunkyo-ku, Tokyo, 112, Japan